Accounting and Finance

MARKET LEADER

Business English

Sara Helm

PEARSON

Longman

FT

FINANCIAL
TIMES

Pearson Education Limited

Edinburgh Gate
Harlow
Essex CM20 2JE
England
and Associated Companies throughout the world.

www.pearsonlongman.com

First published 2010

ARP impression 98

ISBN 978-1-408-22002-3

Set in Metaplus, Times & ITC Cheltenham
Printed in Great Britain by Ashford Colour Press Ltd

Acknowledgements

This series was developed and written by consultants working with LTS Training and Consulting, Bath, a specialist language and intercultural training company.

The author would like to thank the following for their kind help and feedback during the writing and checking process:
Maria Ahnmark, Annagret Rump, Ellen-Hoy Petersen, Cyril Bekkers, Stephan Heil. A very big thank-you goes to Christian 'for your endless patience and excellent culinary skills'.

The author and publishers are grateful to the following teachers who reported on earlier drafts of this material: Christine Thuillier and Uwe Schiffke.

We are grateful to the following for permission to reproduce copyright material:

Text

Extract in Unit 4 from Annual Report & Accounts, 2008, HSBC, Reproduced with permission from HSBC Holdings plc; Extract in Unit 18 from Audit report on company financial statements (of Vodafone Group plc by Deloitte Touche), 19 May 2009, http://www.vodafone.com/static/annual_report/financials/audit_report_comp_fin_statements.html, granted with permission from Deloitte & Touche LLP.

The Financial Times

Extract in Unit 1 adapted from 'Accountancy: Business skills and mobility give you the edge', *The Financial Times*, 16 June 2008 (Newing, R.), copyright © Financial Times Ltd; Extract in Unit 2 adapted from 'Professional bodies: raised profiles rather than world domination', *The Financial Times*, 2 September 2008 (Hughes, J.), copyright © Financial Times Ltd; Extract in Unit 5 adapted from 'Pearson upbeat on trading', *The Financial Times*, 19 January 2009 (Edgecliffe-Johnson, A.), copyright © Financial Times Ltd; Exhibit 6 adapted from 'IASB questions relaxing of fair-value accounting', *The Financial Times*, 7 November 2008 (Hughes, J.), copyright © Financial Times Ltd; Extract in Unit 6 adapted from 'IASB chairman warns on risk to rule', *The Financial Times*, 11 November 2008 (Hughes, J.), copyright © Financial Times Ltd; Extract in Unit 7 adapted from 'China: Desperate rush for entrance. How to do well in China', *The Financial Times*, 25 July 2007 (Tucker, S.), copyright © Financial Times Ltd; Extract in Unit 8 adapted from 'Raising funds for schemes and dream', *The Financial Times*, 21 June 2005 (Richard, D.), copyright © Financial Times Ltd; Extract in Unit 9 adapted from 'Porsche spice', *The Financial Times*, 18 February 2009, copyright © Financial Times Ltd; Extract in Unit 10 adapted from 'Counters face up to green beans', *The Financial Times*, 1 September 2008 (Bruce, R.), copyright © Financial Times Ltd; Extract in Unit 11 adapted from 'Investing in doing good can be good risk management', *The Financial Times*, 25 August 2008 (Clegg, A.), copyright © Financial Times Ltd; Exhibit 12 adapted from 'Scandal raises questions about disclosure rules', *The Financial Times*, 30 January 2009 (Leahy, J.), copyright © Financial Times Ltd; Extract in Unit 13 adapted from 'Rating the credibility of credit agencies', *The Financial Times*, 16 November 2007 (Moore, E.), copyright © Financial Times Ltd; Extract in Unit 14 adapted from 'A responsible approach to insolvency', *The Financial Times*, 5 April 2008 (Moules, M.), copyright © Financial Times Ltd; Extract in Unit 15 adapted from 'Evidence triggered Crosby's departure', *The Financial Times*, 11 February 2009 (Croft, J.), copyright © Financial Times Ltd; Extract in Unit 16 adapted from 'Scary jargon in a jittery market', *The Financial Times*, 1 January 2008 (Hughes, J.), copyright © Financial Times Ltd; Extract in Unit 17 adapted from 'Professional liability: Hard-won solution faces threat from US', *The Financial Times*, 2 September 2008 (Bruce, R.), copyright © Financial Times Ltd.

In some instances we have been unable to trace the owners of copyright material, and we would appreciate any information that would enable us to do so.

Photos

The publisher would like to thank the following for their kind permission to reproduce their photographs:

(Key: b-bottom; c-centre; l-left; r-right; t-top)

Alamy Images: imagebroker 5; Nigel Reed QEDimages 9; **DK Images**: Paul Wilkinson 37; **Getty Images**: Manny Ceneta 25; **Rob Maidment**: 21; **iStockphoto**: 57; Robert Churchill 29; Michael Utech 41; Steve Vanhorn 49; Rudyanto Wijaya 65; **PhotoDisc**: 13; **Photolibrary.com**: MIXA Co. Ltd. 3; Radius Images 33; Reuters: Jonathan Evans 61; **Rex Features**: Ray Tang 53; **shutterstock**: Mikhail Levit 69; **STILL Pictures The Whole Earth Photo Library**: Joerg Boethling 45

Cover photo © **Getty Images**/Robin MacDougall

Every effort has been made to trace the copyright holders and we apologise in advance for any unintentional omissions. We would be pleased to insert the appropriate acknowledgement in any subsequent edition of this publication.

Project managed by Chris Hartley

Contents

Developing global professionals

This unit looks at the broad range of work skills that the modern accountant needs.

Discuss these questions.

1 In your country, what process do you have to go through in order to be able to work as an accountant?
2 Briefly describe any national accountancy qualifications which exist in your country.

A **Understanding the main points**

Read the article on the opposite page and say whether these statements are true (T) or false (F). Identify the part of the article that gives this information. Correct the false ones.

1 Most accountants work for accountancy firms.
2 There are a number of different specialist areas in accounting.
3 Accountancy firms only operate in their domestic market.
4 Accountancy training is mainly organised locally.
5 With a recognised accountancy qualification, you are sufficiently trained for the rest of your working career.
6 IFAC does not expect accountants to get any further training once they have obtained their initial accountancy qualification.
7 Giving its accountants business-skills training can have a serious impact on a firms' success.

B **Understanding details**

Read the article again and answer these questions.

1 Which phrase in paragraph F has the same meaning as *the edge* in the title?
2 What are the three main advantages of an employee who holds a recognised accountancy qualification?
3 Why do accountants generally train in their own country?
4 How does IFAC describe itself?
5 Which two broad sets of skills do large accountancy firms value as much as the purely technical accounting skills?
6 What does KPMG see as being the most important asset in its accountants?
7 Which major barrier to this does KPMG's Senior Training Manager mention?
8 Which markets would currently benefit from having more accountants trained to a high level?
9 Which attributes do employers need their internationally mobile employees to share?
10 What sort of economic benefits would a stronger accountancy profession bring to developing countries, according to ACCA's Chief Executive?

Business skills give you the edge

by Rod Newing

A Anybody can call themselves an accountant, but a recognised qualification generally guarantees proper training, experience and professional standards. Most accountants work in-house for companies or organisations in the private, public or voluntary sectors. Those employed by accountancy firms, on the other hand, usually specialise in very specific areas, such as auditing, taxation, insolvency or forensic accounting. Naturally, each specialism has different training requirements.

B Despite the existence of global accounting practices serving global clients, the accountancy bodies that oversee training are almost entirely domestic and serve the needs of their domestic market.

C Although the widespread adoption of international accounting standards is making training easier, taxation is a national issue. Therefore, accountancy training naturally tends to occur at a national level. 'We are not educating accountants to work anywhere in the world, but to work in their own national environment,' says Jim Sylph, Executive Director of Professional Standards at the International Federation of Accountants (IFAC).

D IFAC describes itself as 'the global organisation for the accountancy profession'. It has 2.5 million members from all areas of the profession, belonging to 157 member and affiliated bodies and accountancy associations, from all over the world.

E But accountancy training is not just about the initial qualification. The big challenge is keeping accountants up to date in a changing world. To support its members, IFAC sets very broad standards for education programmes, including continuing professional education and lifelong learning.

F The current trend is to emphasise strategy and management over the purely technical subjects, because strategic and managerial skills can give the big global practices a competitive advantage.

G In this way, at Pricewaterhouse-Coopers (PwC), the concept of the 'business adviser' runs right through from newly qualified accountants to partners. This includes skills such as managing teams, and coaching and appraising people. Business and relationship skills have huge financial implications. Indeed, they often determine the length of time that the business relationship between an accountancy firm and its customers exists.

H Similarly, global training at KPMG concentrates on values, skills and behaviours. However, KPMG's main strategic focus is the mobility of its workforce, and it views the lack of portability of national qualifications as the main barrier to this. 'It presents challenges within the profession,' says Michael Walby, Senior Training Manager at KPMG. 'We need to be able to get our resource to the opportunities, irrespective of geographical boundaries. The profession needs to work together across the various institutes to take advantage of future opportunities.'

I 'If you get training right, it can make a significant difference to competitive advantage,' says Ms Kilbride, Associate Partner for Global Learning at Deloitte. This is especially the case in small or emerging markets that are growing rapidly. They face challenges to consistency and quality because of a rapid influx of people.

J According to Mr Blewitt, Chief Executive of the Association of Chartered Certified Accountants (ACCA), increasingly employers want people who can move around the world with a common accounting language and set of standards and ethics. He states, 'There is an inexhaustible demand from developing nations. With a qualified accountancy profession, these countries will continue to be able to attract inward investment and aid from agencies such as the World Bank.'

FT

VOCABULARY

A Definitions

Paragraph A lists four accountancy specialisms. Match these words and phrases from the article (1–4) with their meanings (a–d).

1	auditing	a)	when a company's financial records are officially checked because illegal activity is suspected
2	tax accounting	b)	an accountant working in this area acts for a person or company that is no longer able to pay their debts or a company whose liabilities exceed its assets
3	insolvency	c)	preparing a person's or company's financial information in order to calculate the proportion of their profit which they must pay to their government
4	forensic accounting	d)	checking an organisation's activities or performance or examining a person's or organisation's accounts to make sure that they are true and honest

B Word search

Read paragraphs G and H again and match each of these nouns or noun phrases with either PwC or KPMG.

1 business adviser concept *PwC*
2 mobility
3 values and behaviours
4 team-management skills
5 coaching
6 employee appraisal
7 relationship skills

C Sentence completion

Use words and phrases from Exercises A and B to complete these sentences.

1 Due to a sharp drop in sales, the company was not able to pay its creditors and eventually entered into ....

2 Accountants need to deal with clients, so it is important for them to have .... skills as well as technical ones.

3 It is important to have ....-........ skills if you are going to be responsible for groups of employees.

4 Accountants involved in .... check that their clients' financial statements present a true and honest picture of the company.

5 The company was suspected of being dishonest in its financial reporting, so the .... accountants were called in to investigate its dealings.

6 Accountants need to develop .... skills in order to give appropriate feedback to the teams they manage.

D   Word partnerships

Match the sentence halves to make sentences similar to ones in the article.

1	Global accounting practices serve	a)	a wide range of education programmes.
2	A recognised qualification guarantees	b)	a significant difference to competitive advantage.
3	Accountancy bodies that oversee training serve	c)	global clients.
4	IFAC provides	d)	challenges to consistency and quality.
5	Good training can make	e)	proper training.
6	Emerging markets face	f)	the needs of their domestic market.

E   Linking ideas

1   Find five words or phrases in the article which express contrast or similarity. Identify the sentences in which they appear and state which idea they express.

    EXAMPLE: *Anybody can call themselves an accountant, but a recognised qualification generally guarantees proper training, experience and professional standards. (lines 1–5)*
'But' expresses contrast.

2   Write five sentences of your own, using the linking words and phrases you found in Exercise 1.

F   Understanding expressions

Choose the best explanation for each phrase from the article.

1   '... not just about the *initial* qualification.' (lines 39–40)
    a)   occurring at the end
    b)   occurring at the beginning

2   '... have huge financial *implications*.' (lines 60–61)
    a)   consequences
    b)   difficulties

3   'There is an *inexhaustible* demand ...' (lines 96–97)
    a)   never-ending
    b)   enormous

OVER TO YOU

1   Do an Internet search of the accountancy firms mentioned in the article. Which areas of professional training do they provide, and which firm looks the most interesting to work for? Write a short report.

2   Vocabulary Exercise B lists several non-technical aspects of accountancy work. Explain what they might involve and whether you think they make the job more interesting.

3   Which of the accountancy specialisms mentioned in the article do you think would be the most interesting to work in? Explain your ideas in a short presentation.

Establishing the profession worldwide

This unit looks at the development of the accounting profession around the world.

Discuss these questions.

1   Which professional accounting organisations operate in your country?
    Are they local or international?
2   What advantages are there to both employers and employees in having links with professional accounting bodies?

READING

A   **Understanding the main points**

Read the article on the opposite page and answer these questions.
Identify the part of the article that gives this information.

1   How are some of the UK accounting bodies helping to develop the accountancy profession overseas with local institutes?
2   What does ACCA think about the fact that some of the accounting organisations it is supporting will most probably become its competitors in the future?
3   As well as accountancy, which other area of training has CIMA identified as being essential to overseas accountants?
4   Robert Jelly mentions that there is a growing need for a common set of accounting qualifications around the world. What reasons does he give for this?
5   Which set of accounting standards is in the process of being adopted by over a hundred countries?
6   What benefit would a well-established accounting profession bring to developing economies?
7   In spite of UK help, what is the most important factor in the development of a strong accounting profession in developing countries, according to Neil Wallace?

B   **Understanding details**

Read the article again and answer these questions.
Identify the part of the article that gives this information.

1   What proportion of ACCA's members are registered outside the UK?
2   Which programme do CIMA and ICAEW's projects in Bangladesh belong to?
3   Which Bangladeshi institute is CIMA helping?
4   In which developing regions is the accountancy profession becoming more important?
5   What sort of jobs do the visiting Bangladeshi accountants have?
6   What does Anton Colella, Chief Executive of ICAS, want to see happening in Eastern Europe?
7   Which organisation has been established in Kazakhstan?

Professional bodies: global profiles

by Jennifer Hughes

A In Chartered Accountants' Hall, there is a memorial to past presidents of the Institute of Chartered Accountants in England and Wales (ICAEW). Names
5 such as Waterhouse, Coopers, Peat and Young display the largely British roots of the profession.

B But these days, the ICAEW and other UK accounting bodies are look-
10 ing overseas. 'Accountancy is an international business,' says Vernon Soare of the ICAEW. 'We are developing to support our members and the firms they work in.' Today, there is
15 much talk of partnerships with local institutes and developing an international reputation for the qualifications they offer.

C Over half of the Association of
20 Chartered Certified Accountants' (ACCA) 122,500 members are registered overseas. ACCA feels that work that helps the standing of the profession across the world helps its members,
25 even if it is supporting bodies that will eventually become competitors.

D Both the ICAEW and the Chartered Institute of Management Accountants (CIMA) are working on World Bank
30 projects in Bangladesh to develop professional services to support its economy and businesses. CIMA is studying the accounting profession and the operations of the Institute of
35 Cost and Management Accountants of Bangladesh.

E CIMA is also establishing joint ventures with a number of overseas institutes and looking at local language
40 training. 'The main part of our growth strategy is employer-led. We listen to them carefully. There has been a huge shift in the finance function. Finance processes are being outsourced [to a
45 variety of countries], so there is an increasing need for common qualifications around the world,' says Robert Jelly, Director of Education at CIMA.

F In the UK, the ICAEW has hosted
50 Bangladeshi accountants working towards the Institute's certificate in International Financial Reporting Standards (IFRS). These are the accounting rules now accepted or in

55 the process of being adopted by more than 100 countries. The group includes academics, regulators and government officials. 'They are not simply learning the technical side, they are learning
60 how to teach it and pass it on,' says Mr Soare. The aim is to develop a stronger accounting profession in the country to help build a stronger economic system.

G Another exciting area is Eastern
65 Europe and central Asia. The Institute of Chartered Accountants of Scotland (ICAS) is working in Armenia and Kazakhstan to bring together Russian speakers from across the region to
70 help develop the profession and to discuss IFRS.

H 'It is a fast-developing part of the world. We have a good reputation in the region due to the development work
75 we have already done there,' says Anton Colella, Chief Executive of ICAS. 'We want to build strong national institutes. The demands and pressures on the global profession
80 are increasing, particularly in developing nations, where IFRS and international audit standards are proving very challenging.'

I But all the institutes insist the UK
85 profession is not looking for world domination. 'There is always going to be a need for local control. You need to understand local customs, to build groups of professionals who have
90 loyalty to each other and to their local profession,' says Neil Wallace, Director of International Services at ICAS. 'Take Kazakhstan. It now has a chamber of auditors, and the profes-
95 sion is developing alongside the economy, something all developing countries need.'

FT

C ### How the text is organised

What do these words refer to in the article?

1 they (line 18)
2 its (line 24)
3 its (line 31)

4 them (line 42)
5 these (line 53)
6 it (line 72)

VOCABULARY

A **Word search**

Find words or phrases in the article which fit these meanings.

1 An area of work that needs advanced education and specific training (paragraph A)

accountancy p........

2 Official organisations which represent people of a particular profession (paragraph B)

a) accountancy b........   b) accountancy i........

3 The set of new accounting rules that over 100 countries have adopted or are in the process of adopting (paragraph F)

I........ F........ R........ S........

4 A person or organisation chosen by the government to ensure that an industry or system operates legally or fairly (paragraph F)

r........

5 Someone who has a responsible position in a government organisation (paragraph F)

g........ o........

6 Official body of auditors, who check that a company's financial report is true and honest (paragraph I)

c........ of auditors

B **Vocabulary development**

Find different forms of the word *develop* in the article and use them to complete these sentences.

1 ICAS is working in Armenia and Kazakhstan to help .... the profession.

2 Several institutes have been doing .... work in Eastern Europe.

3 .... nations need a strong accountancy profession.

4 Accountancy is a fast-........ profession.

5 There is much talk of .... an international reputation for the qualifications that overseas institutes offer.

C **Sentence completion**

Use words and phrases from Exercises A and B to complete these sentences.

1 In the future, many accountants in developing countries will produce company accounts which comply with ....

2 Although developing countries need international help to establish the .... in their countries, success will depend mainly on having strong local control.

3 Many .... are working hard with these countries to develop local qualifications with an international reputation.

4 Some countries even have a .... of .... for the first time.

5 It is equally important that their ...., who are responsible for making sure that an industry or system works legally or fairly, have a good understanding of accounting.

6 The international accountancy profession is .... fast.

D **Word partnerships**

Match the sentence halves to make sentences similar to ones in the article.

1	ICAEW is developing	a)	joint ventures with a number of overseas institutes.
2	CIMA is studying	b)	its members and the firms they work in.
3	CIMA is establishing	c)	to discuss IFRS.
4	Finance processes are	d)	the accounting profession of Bangladesh.
5	The demands and pressures on the global profession	e)	being outsourced overseas to a variety of countries.
6	ICAS is bringing Russian speakers together	f)	are increasing.
7	International audit standards are proving challenging	g)	in developing nations.

E **Understanding expressions**

Choose the best explanation for each phrase from the article.

1 'The main part of our growth strategy is *employer-led*.' (lines 40–41)
   a) followed by employers
   b) heavily influenced by employers

2 'There has been *a huge shift* in the finance function.' (lines 42–43)
   a) a long working period
   b) a big move

3 'Finance processes are being *outsourced* ...' (lines 43–44)
   a) carried out by another company
   b) carried out by another country

4 'These are the accounting rules now accepted or in the process of being *adopted* by more than 100 countries.' (lines 53–56)
   a) used for the first time
   b) changed

OVER TO YOU

1 In the article, several UK accounting bodies are mentioned. Do an Internet search to find out what they are doing in your country or a country you are interested in. Give a short presentation.

2 What benefits can a strong accounting profession bring to developing countries?
   Think about international trade and stock markets, local economies, companies and employees.
   Write a short report to explain your ideas.

International Financial Reporting Standards

This unit looks at the set of international accounting and reporting rules which is being adopted by a large number of countries.

BEFORE YOU READ

Discuss these questions.

1   Has your country adopted the International Financial Reporting Standards, or is it in the process of doing so? Briefly describe the main aim of this set of standards.

2   For companies which have made the change to the new set of standards, how easy do you think that process was? Can you think of any difficulties they might have encountered? Explain your ideas.

READING

A   **Understanding the main points**

Read the article on the opposite page and say whether these statements are true (T) or false (F). Correct the false ones. Identify the part of the article that gives this information.

1   The European changeover to International Financial Reporting Standards went as expected.

2   CEOs need to fully understand how these accounting and reporting changes could affect the way their financial results look to outsiders.

3   The changeover to IFRS only involved changing a few numbers in the accounts of the companies concerned.

4   Once companies had understood which accounting policies they had to change, the major problems were over.

5   The changeover experience was the same for each of the companies involved.

6   Many European countries' old reporting standards had been designed mainly with their respective tax authorities in mind.

B   **Understanding details**

Read the article again and answer these questions.

1   There is a pun in the title. Can you explain it?

2   Which expression describes a negative effect on the final accounting report which can occur if a company does not make the necessary changes throughout the whole organisation?

3   How did senior executives at Tomkins have to handle these changes in terms of the outside world?

4   Shortly after the changeover to IFRS, what evidence was there that analysts and investors might not have fully understood the new method of reporting and reacted negatively?

5   Find the phrase in paragraph E which shows that the changes had simply been regarded as a minor technical accounting change.

6   Who was the new reporting system aimed at?

7   In Europe, which type of company generally found the changeover process more difficult?

CEOs need to take account of IFRS

by Jennifer Hughes

A 'No one anticipated how big it was going to be!' says Ken Wild, global International Financial Reporting Standards (IFRS) leader at Deloitte, speaking of the European switch to the new international accounting standards. 'Every company was too late and too slow in preparing – even the good ones.'

B Accounting used to be in the hands of only the bookkeepers and auditors. Not any more. The change in accounting rules has forced many Chief Executive Officers (CEOs) to roll up their sleeves. Even when they have reached the first milestone of the changeover, they need to keep up to date with ongoing developments in IFRS in order to deal with the way their company's financial performance will be viewed from the outside.

C A changeover to IFRS involves far more changes than might at first appear. These range from retraining staff and altering data-collection systems to potentially changing pay policies and adjusting key accounting policies in order to avoid anomalies in the reported accounts. Changing over was more difficult than many originally anticipated. It required a lot of adjustments to the computer information systems to try to build the final financial statements.

D Mark Smith, Director of External Reporting at Tomkins, led his engineering group through the change. 'There were really two phases to the whole project,' he says. 'Firstly, we had to work out which accounting policies had to change. Secondly, we had to understand how to produce the new style of accounts.' The extra disclosure requirements caused headaches. 'It was not necessarily huge additional amounts of data, but the differences in the data which caused problems – collecting it and explaining why you need it.'

E Externally, there were also big challenges. Executives had to educate the market as to what the different numbers meant and prepare investors and analysts for any significant changes. During the UK conversion, PwC staff tracked the share price movements of companies on the first day they reported results under IFRS. 'The moves were normally 1 or 2 per cent, so that is not bad, but that is, in fact, a big deal for something that was promoted as only a change in book keeping,' says Ian Dilks, head of the IFRS conversion team at PwC.

F No two companies go through exactly the same experience, and the extent of the change depends on the complexity of the company. Financial services and multinational firms tend to be at one end of the scale, and small companies that operate only domestically at the other.

G In Europe, the process was complicated further by different accounting rules in each country. Some of these were more geared towards tax collection and required a major reorientation towards capital markets, in line with IFRS.

H Interestingly, European companies with less-developed accounting systems were generally better prepared for the switchover, whereas many UK companies had to rush to work through the unexpected detail of the new requirements. UK accounting was considered quite similar to IFRS. Some companies made the mistake of thinking that the change would be relatively easy.

I 'This is absolutely not just a technical issue,' says Mr Dilks. 'Should CEOs be panicking? No – but neither should they be thinking that they can simply leave this issue to someone else much lower down [their organisation].'

FT

VOCABULARY

A Word search

Find words or phrases in the article which fit these meanings.

1 a) the title of the manager with the greatest authority in the normal everyday management of a company (paragraph B) C........ E........ O........

   b) people who make an official record of all the money paid into and paid out of businesses (paragraph B) b........

   c) person who is in charge of the way a company reports its accounts to the outside world (paragraph D) D........ of E........ R.......

2 a synonym for *profitability* (paragraph B) f........ p........

3 the documents that are produced for investors at the end of the accounting process (paragraph C)

   a) r........ a........   b) f........ f........ s........

4 a synonym for the 'main methods of accounting' (paragraph C) k........ a........ p........

5 things which do not 'fit' in a company's accounts (paragraph C) a........

6 rules which force companies to publish a specific piece of information in their accounts (paragraph D) d........ r........

7 companies can get extra funds by selling shares here (paragraph G) c........ m........

B Word families

Complete the chart with different words and expressions to describe change.

verb	noun
adjust	........¹
........²	alteration
change	change
change over	........³
convert	........⁴
reorient	........⁵
........⁶	switchover

C Sentence completion

Use words and phrases from Exercises A and B to complete these sentences.

1 The .... to the new set of accounting rules by many European companies was much more complicated than they originally thought it would be.

2 Companies had to assess how they would have to .... their accounting and reporting processes.

3 They had to start by adjusting their ....

4 The .... of .... has responsibility for how the company presents its accounts to the public.

5 The public will use the .... to get a picture of the company's financial performance.

6 Companies need to fulfil all of the .... in their reported accounts in order to comply with IFRS.

7 They must be careful not to publish any .... in their accounts.

D **Vocabulary development**

Use the verbs and verb phrases in the box to complete the description of some of the steps involved in the process of changing over to IFRS.

adjust	alter	change	educate	keep up to date with	prepare	produce	retrain	understand

CEOs have to ...

1 .... ongoing developments in IFRS.

2 .... the impact of IFRS on the view of the company's performance from the outside world.

Companies have to ...

3 .... staff.

4 .... data-collection systems.

5 .... pay policies.

6 .... key accounting policies.

Directors of External Reporting have to ...

7 .... the new style of accounts.

CEOs have to ...

8 .... the market about the new style of reporting.

9 .... analysts and investors for any significant changes.

E **Understanding expressions**

Choose the best explanation for each phrase from the article.

1 '... has forced many Chief Executive Officers to *roll up their sleeves*.' (lines 13–15)

   a) start fighting   b) work very hard

2 '... when they have *reached the first milestone* ...' (lines 15–16)

   a) put in place the main parts of the new reporting system
   b) experienced their first problems with the new reporting system

3 '... but that is, in fact, *a big deal* ...' (lines 60–61)

   a) very significant   b) a big business contract

4 '... the *extent* of the change depends on the complexity of the company.' (lines 66–68)

   a) size   b) cost

OVER TO YOU

1 Go to www.IASB.co.uk for an update on accounting standards changes around the world. Discuss how they might affect your country.

2 Write a short report about the advantages to companies around the world of sharing a common set of accounting and reporting standards.

3 Go to www.IFRS.co.uk for further information on the process of changeover to IFRS and how it has affected companies involved. Give a short presentation about a company which has gone through the changeover process.

Annual financial statements

This unit looks at a consolidated income (profit-and-loss) statement and balance sheet of HSBC Holdings plc.

BEFORE YOU READ

Discuss these questions.

1 What are the main items on a bank's a) income statement, b) balance sheet?
2 What do the bank's shareholders mainly look for when reading them?

READING 1

A **Understanding the main points**

Read HSBC's 2007 and 2008 income statement on the opposite page and decide whether these statements are true (T) or false (F). Correct the false ones.
Indicate the line(s) in the statement that give you the answer.

1 In 2008, the total operating income increased slightly on the previous year.
2 Interest expenses fell by a larger amount than the fall in interest from savers' accounts, so the net figure actually went up on the previous year.
3 Trading income rose significantly on the previous year.
4 Employee salaries and bonuses are deducted from the operating profit.
5 The banking group sold off some German regional banks in 2008.
6 The bank's tax bill in 2008 was lower than in the previous year.
7 Earnings per share were significantly reduced on the previous year.

VOCABULARY 1

A **Definitions**

Match these words and phrases from the income statement (1–6) with their meanings (a–f).

1 operating income   a) A part of the profits of the company for a particular period of time that is paid to shareholders for each share that they own
2 depreciation   b) Money earned from a company's normal activities, not including exceptional items
3 goodwill   c) The value that a company has in addition to its assets, such as a good reputation with its customers
4 dividend   d) Profit relating to a company's normal activities of providing goods or services, before tax is deducted
5 operating profit   e) Costs relating to a company's normal activities of providing goods or services
6 operating expense   f) The gradual loss in value of a fixed asset that wears out over a number of years or needs to be replaced regularly

Summary Consolidated Income Statement

US$m

	2008	2007
Interest income	91,301	92,359
Interest expense	(48,738)	(54,564)
Net interest income	42,563	37,795
Fee income	24,764	26,337
Fee expense	(4,740)	(4,335)
Net fee income	20,024	22,002
Trading income excluding net interest income	847	4,458
Net interest income on trading activities	5,713	5,376
Net trading income	6,560	9,834
Changes in fair value of long-term debt issued and related derivatives	6,679	2,812
Net income/(expense) from other financial instruments designated at fair value	(2,827)	1,271
Net income from financial instruments designated at fair value	3,852	4,083
Gains less losses from financial investments	197	1,956
Gains arising from dilution of interests in associates	–	1,092
Dividend income	272	324
Net earned insurance premiums	10,850	9,076
Gains on disposal of French regional banks	2,445	–
Other operating income	1,808	1,439
Total operating income	88,571	87,601
Net insurance claims incurred and movement in liabilities to policyholders	(6,889)	(8,608)
Net operating income before loan impairment charges and other credit-risk provisions	81,682	78,993
Loan impairment charges and other credit-risk provisions	(24,937)	(17,242)
Net operating income	56,745	61,751
Employee compensation and benefits	(20,792)	(21,334)
General and administrative expenses	(15,260)	(15,294)
Depreciation and impairment of property, plant and equipment	(1,750)	(1,714)
Goodwill impairment	(10,564)	–
Amortisation and impairment of intangible assets	(733)	(700)
Total operating expenses	(49,099)	(39,042)
Operating profit	7,646	22,709
Share of profit in associates and joint ventures	1,661	1,503
Profit before tax	9,307	24,212
Tax expense	(2,809)	(3,757)
Profit for the year	6,498	20,455
Profit attributable to shareholders of the parent company	5,728	19,133
Profit attributable to minority interests	770	1,322
US$		
Basic earnings per ordinary share	0.47	1.65
Diluted earnings per ordinary share	0.47	1.63
Dividends per ordinary share	0.93	0.87

Reproduced with permission from HSBC Holdings plc *Annual Report and Accounts 2008*

READING 2

A Understanding the main points

Read the balance sheet on the opposite page and say whether these statements are true (T) or false (F). Correct the false ones. Indicate the line(s) in the statement that give you the answer.

1 The bank more than doubled its cash deposits in 2008.

2 Customers had more money in savings than in the previous year.

3 The bank lent a lot more money to customers and other banks compared to the previous year.

4 The bank's derivatives increased dramatically in 2008.

5 The bank's pension liabilities went up significantly in 2008.

6 Shareholders' equity grew significantly on the previous year.

7 The value of the bank's intangible assets decreased in 2008.

8 The bank's balance sheet grew in 2008. However, the bank's 'other reserves' ended the year as a negative figure.

VOCABULARY 2

A Word search

Find words in the balance sheet which fit these meanings.

1 things which belong to a business which have the value or power to create money, such as machinery

a........

2 amounts of money owed by a business to a supplier or lender

l........

3 money which is lent or borrowed

l........

4 money set aside for a future expense (such as debts which a company's customers fail to pay)

p........

5 shares which have been issued and for which the company is demanding payment

c........-u........s........c........

6 the capital that a company has from shares rather than from loans

e........

7 less than half a company's shares, or fewer shares than the largest shareholder

m........i........

8 the part of a company's profits from previous years which have not been paid to investors

r........

OVER TO YOU

2008 was a less profitable year for HSBC Holdings plc than 2007 due to the economic and banking crisis. However, several other British banking groups suffered much more severely. Do an Internet search to find out which banks were worst affected and write a short report.

Summary Consolidated Balance Sheet

US$m

US$m	2008	2007
ASSETS		
Cash and balances at central banks	52,396	21,765
Items in the course of collection from other banks	6,003	9,777
Hong Kong Government certificates of indebtedness	15,358	13,893
Trading assets	427,329	445,968
Financial assets designated at fair value	28,533	41,564
Derivatives	494,876	187,854
Loans and advances to banks	153,766	237,366
Loans and advances to customers	932,868	981,548
Financial investments	300,235	283,000
Interests in associates and joint ventures	11,537	10,384
Goodwill and intangible assets	27,357	39,689
Property, plant and equipment	14,025	15,694
Other assets	37,822	39,493
Current tax assets	2,552	896
Deferred tax assets	7,011	5,284
Prepayments and accrued income	15,797	20,091
Total assets	**2,527,465**	2,354,266
LIABILITIES AND EQUITY		
Liabilities		
Hong Kong currency notes in circulation	15,358	13,893
Deposits by banks	130,084	132,181
Customer accounts	1,115,327	1,096,140
Items in the course of transmission to other banks	7,232	8,672
Trading liabilities	247,652	314,580
Financial liabilities designated at fair value	74,587	89,939
Derivatives	487,060	183,393
Debt securities in issue	179,693	246,579
Retirement benefit liabilities	3,888	2,893
Other liabilities	72,384	35,013
Current tax liabilities	1,822	2,559
Liabilities under insurance contracts	43,683	42,606
Accruals and deferred income	15,448	21,766
Provisions	1,730	1,958
Deferred tax liabilities	1,855	1,859
Subordinated liabilities	29,433	24,819
Total liabilities	**2,427,236**	2,218,850
Equity		
Called-up share capital	6,053	5,915
Share premium account	8,463	8,134
Other equity instruments	2,133	–
Other reserves	(3,747)	33,014
Retained earnings	80,689	81,097
Total shareholders' equity	**93,591**	128,160
Minority interests	6,638	7,256
Total equity	**100,229**	135,416
Total equity and liabilities	**2,527,465**	2,354,266

Reproduced with permission from HSBC Holdings plc *Annual Report and Accounts 2008*

Company performance

This unit looks at a company's recent performance and its performance forecast.

Discuss these questions.

1   Companies publish forecasts of their expected results. Who are these forecasts aimed at, and why do companies publish these regularly?

2   Why is it important for companies not to overestimate their future earnings?

A   **Understanding the main points**

Read the article on the opposite page and say whether these statements are true (T) or false (F). Correct the false ones. Identify the part of the article that gives this information.

1   Pearson's results were worse than expected in 2008.

2   Some of Pearson's competitors did better than expected in that year.

3   Pearson operates in the travel and tourism market.

4   Pearson owns the *Financial Times* newspaper

5   It expected 2009 to be a challenging year for some of its markets.

6   Not all of the analysts who studied this market were quite as convinced that the future looked so rosy.

7   The economic downturn may actually have improved Pearson's sales in 2008.

B   **Understanding details**

Read the article again and answer these questions.

1   What figure had Pearson's adjusted earnings per share originally been estimated at?

2   What price did Pearson's shares reach by the end of the year?

3   At the beginning of the year, what size of drop in US state schools' educational materials spending did rival publisher McGraw-Hill forecast?

4   Which two financial factors had contributed to Pearson's better-than-expected performance?

5   Which two negative factors had analysts been concerned about before Christmas?

6   What percentage of Pearson Education's income depends on the US educational market?

7   Which division of Pearson did not perform as well in the final three months of 2008 as it had in the previous nine months?

8   Which Pearson division's performance did not surprise anyone?

Pearson upbeat on trading

by Andrew Edgecliffe-Johnson

A Pearson met or exceeded its previous guidance for 2008 in all its businesses, the publisher said this week. This was in marked contrast to a number
5 of 'bearish' announcements from rival educational, book and newspaper companies. The owner of the *Financial Times* said, in a trading update, that it expected full-year earnings growth
10 of around 20 per cent, indicating that adjusted earnings per share could advance from 46.7p to about 56p, ahead of consensus forecasts of 51p.

B 'We are naturally cautious about the
15 economic environment, but we take confidence from our performance in 2008,' said Dame Marjorie Scardino, Chief Executive. 'Some of our markets will be tough this year, and we are
20 managing the company accordingly,' she added. However, Pearson's strategy, past investments and resilience would enable it 'to take full advantage of the opportunities this environment
25 gives us to build our business and gain [market] share'.

C Pearson's shares closed up 27p at 625p. Pearson's statement stood in clear contrast to recent comments by
30 some rivals. McGraw-Hill, the US educational publisher, cautioned in January that spending by states on elementary- to high-school materials had slumped since August and might
35 fall by 10–15 per cent this year.

D This statement marks the second time in three months that Pearson has indicated that its earnings would be above consensus levels. It noted
40 that earnings had benefited from the strength of the dollar and a tax rate towards the lower end of a previous 27–29-per-cent guidance range.

E Analysts had also been prepared for
45 poor Christmas sales from consumer book publishers, since Borders, the US book retailer, said its holiday sales had fallen by 11 per cent. Analysts were also worried about the impact
50 of a weak advertising market on the FT Group.

F Simon Baker of Credit Suisse commented, 'It is good news, but there are some question marks. Pearson is
55 a late-cycle company, and if the good news now is coming from market share increases, from the tax charge and the strong dollar, people are generally going to be cautious about as-
60 suming all that will continue.' Alex de Groote, analyst at Panmure Gordon, stated 'There are certainly no new horror stories, but I remain concerned about exposure to the education
65 market in the US.'

G Pearson's statement highlighted the strength in its historically counter-cyclical US higher-education business. This has benefited from a contracting
70 job market, which has encouraged more people to invest in continuing education rather than looking for employment. Growth in the inter-national education business helped
75 offset 'some weakness' in the US school publishing market, which accounts for approximately one-fifth of Pearson Education, and slightly more than 10 per cent of group revenues.

H FT Publishing, which includes the *FT*, business magazines and online brands such as Mergermarket, saw an advertising slowdown in the fourth quarter, but produced 'good sales and
85 profit growth' for the full year.

I Penguin Group UK (which incorp-orates famous brands such as the *Rough Guides* to travel, Penguin Classics and the Puffin and Ladybird children's
90 books) performed 'in line with expectations', Pearson said.

FT

VOCABULARY

A Vocabulary development

1 When someone expects prices on a financial market to rise or economic activity to increase, they are said to be *bullish*. Find a word in paragraph A which has the opposite meaning.

2 Complete the chart with words from paragraph G of the article.

adjective	noun
growing	 1
.... 2	contraction
strong	 3
weak	 4

B Word search

Find words or phrases in the article which precede a figure to show it is an approximation.

1 *a*........ (paragraph A)

2 *a*........ (paragraph A)

3 *a*........ (paragraph G)

4 *s*........ *m*........ *t*........ (paragraph G)

C Definitions

Find words or phrases in the article which match these meanings.

1 forecast (*noun*) (paragraph A) *g*........

2 latest business information (paragraph A) *t*........ *u*........

3 good performance under difficult conditions (paragraph B) *r*........

4 a market which takes time to react to changing economic conditions (*adjective*) (paragraph F)
   l........-*c*........

5 not following the normal pattern of business activity (*adjective*) (paragraph G)
   c........-*c*........

D Word partnerships

Match the verbs (1–4) with the nouns (a–d) to make word partnerships from the article.
Then match each word partnership with a definition (i–iv).

1 meet a) guidance i) to take some of its competitors' part of the business

2 offset b) guidance ii) to reach forecast targets

3 gain c) weakness iii) to do better than originally forecast

4 exceed d) market share iv) to make up for areas which are not as successful

E **Understanding expressions**

1 Complete these sentences from the article.

1 The owner of the *Financial Times* said, in a trading update, that it .... full-year earnings growth of around 20 per cent. (paragraph A)

2 ... indicating that adjusted earnings per share .... advance from 46.7p to about 56p, ahead of consensus forecasts of 51p. (paragraph A)

3 'Some of our markets .... be tough this year ...' (paragraph B)

4 ... spending by states [...] had slumped since August and .... fall by 10–15 per cent this year. (paragraph C)

2 Use the missing phrases from Exercise 1 to complete this chart, according to the degree of certainty they express.

possible	relatively confident	certain
.... 1 2	 3	 4

F **Sentence completion**

Use words and phrases from Exercises A–E to complete these sentences.

1 Companies and their investors are always happy to announce in their .... that they have .... or exceeded their guidance on future performance.

2 In an economic downturn, it can help if some of the markets a company operates in are ....-........ . This can help to .... any weakness in its operations.

3 These markets might be .... markets which the company has not been as active in up to now.

4 They tend to predict that the earnings per share .... or might go up, unless they are very sure that they will, in which case they state that they are .... to go up.

5 They rarely give an exact figure. Instead, they use phrases like '........' or '........ ....'.

OVER TO YOU

1 Imagine that you are a radio broadcaster delivering a financial update. Present Pearson's performance report as a short presentation. Pay careful attention to the pronunciation of the numbers contained in the report.

2 Choose a specific market or sector and write a short report comparing the performance forecasts of two or more competitors in it.

3 Do a *Financial Times* online search at www.FT.com. Type the word 'performance forecast' into the search engine. Choose a company you are interested in and write a short summary of its performance report.

Accounting for banks

This unit looks at how an accounting standard for European banks was changed in 2008 in response to the global banking crisis.

Discuss these questions.

1   What sort of problems can arise if the amount of money that banks are allowed to lend to their private and business customers suddenly becomes restricted?

2   Briefly describe the crisis in the international banking system which began in 2007.

> The amount of money that a bank can lend to its customers depends on the amount of capital reserves it holds. Therefore, if the value of a bank's assets decrease, the amount of money it can lend also goes down.

A   Understanding the main points

Read the article on the opposite page and say whether these statements are true (T) or false (F). Identify the part of the article that gives this information.

1   The European banks changed the way they valued certain types of asset in late 2008.

2   In Sir David Tweedie's opinion, this weakened banking accounting practices.

3   He said that the overruling of the IASB by politicians posed no particular threat to the gradual move towards a global set of accounting rules.

4   The change had the effect of increasing the book valuation of certain bank assets.

5   European banks originally used the amortised cost system of accounting to value their assets.

6   These changes came about after a sharp upturn in the economy.

7   In Sir David Tweedie's opinion, a change in the way regulators calculated a bank's lending ability would have been better than a change in banking accounting and reporting practice.

B   Understanding details

Read the article again and answer these questions.

1   Which institution was Sir David Tweedie representing?

2   Which institution imposed the new accounting rules?

3   In one week alone, by how much were the troubled European banks able to increase their asset values?

4   In that week, how much in losses did they save?

5   Which country's regulators had been moving closer to using the IASB accounting rules before the change?

6   What did the new amortised cost valuation rules require banks to do?

7   What was the banks' criticism of the old rules?

IASB questions relaxing of fair-value accounting

by Jennifer Hughes

A European banks' accounting practices deteriorated as a result of the relaxing of fair-value accounting standards in late 2008, according to Sir David Tweedie,
5 Head of the International Accounting Standards Board (IASB). After a battle with the European Commission in October 2008, the IASB was forced to change its rules without consultation.
10 He warned that any further interfering in accounting rules by politicians would risk destroying the long-running project towards developing a single global set of accounting rules.

B The change helped troubled European banks reclassify some of their assets and avoid a hit to their earnings. In a single week, more than €113bn ($144bn) was moved under the new rules. This saved
20 more than €3bn in losses from banks' revenues.

C The adjustment allowed banks to account for more of their assets using the amortised cost method. This way,
25 asset gains are reported steadily over the lifetime of the financial instrument. Therefore, during a period of market volatility, the reduced market value of an asset at any specific point in time is
30 not taken into account.

D The change came as the US Securities and Exchange Commission was close to releasing its own detailed 'roadmap' of how it proposed to shift from US
35 accounting rules to the international system – a move that would effectively 'cement' the use of the IASB's rules as the single worldwide accounting

language. However, Sir David explain-
40 ed that in order to create a level playing field for the international banking sector, the IASB had made its change only because its US counterpart was not yet in a position to do so.

E The new rules would require banks to disclose any assets valued at amortised cost. However, Sir David argued that the original 'fair-value' system, which led banks to write down hundreds of
50 billions in the value of their holdings as markets plunged in 2008, had its benefits. It had at least forced regulators and executives to face the problems head on, rather than hiding from them.

F He warned that in spite of the added disclosures, using amortised cost would still allow banks to rely to heavily on their own judgement in valuing their holdings – a practice he questioned.
60 'They bought these assets originally and thought they were going to be fine. Well, they weren't. So how accurate is their long-term assessment?'

G On the other hand, many banks had
65 complained that fair-value accounting was pro-cyclical because it helped to exaggerate the impact of a downturn. They had criticised the rules for reducing their capital reserves by making them
70 report losses on assets which they continued to hold and had no intention of selling.

H Regulators closely link their assessment of a bank's reserves with its
75 published accounts. These watchdogs can suddenly require a bank to hold more capital when markets are falling – at the very point when it is hardest for it to do so. Sir David argued that it
80 would be better if regulators changed the way they used a bank's accounts to calculate its capital needs.

I The changes created a storm in the accounting and regulatory world. Some
85 observers warned that by giving in to political pressure, led by European opposition to the current fair-value rules, the IASB had permanently damaged its credibility.

FT

C **How the text is organised**

What do these words refer to in the article?

1 their (line 58)   4 they (line 62)

2 they (line 60)   5 their (line 63)

3 they (line 61)   6 its (line 82)

VOCABULARY

A Definitions

Match these accounting terms (1–2) with their meanings (a–b).
Then match them with the correct chart (i–ii).

1 fair-value asset valuation

2 amortised cost asset valuation

a) An asset's market value at any specific point in time is not taken into account.
It is assumed to increase steadily over the asset's lifetime.

b) An asset's valuation at any specific point in time is based on the amount of
money that could be obtained if the asset were sold at that time.

B Synonyms

Find words or phrases in the article which mean the same as these words and phrases.

1 a change (paragraph C)   a........

2 to change (paragraph D)   to s........

3 judgement (paragraph F)   a........

4 regulators (paragraph H)   w........

5 cash and easily liquidated assets
that a bank must hold to satisfy
stock-exchange regulations (paragraph H)   c........ n........

C Opposites

Find words or phrases in the article which have the opposite meaning to these words.

1 improved (paragraph A)   5 to keep secret (paragraph E)
d........   to d........

2 healthy (paragraph B)   6 to mark up (paragraph E)
t........   to w........ d........

3 market stability (paragraph C) 7 rose sharply (paragraph E)
m........ v........   p........

4 increased market value (paragraph C)   8 an upturn (paragraph G)
r........ m........ v........   a d........

D **Sentence completion**

Use words and phrases from Exercises A–C in the correct form to complete these sentences.

1 The banks prefer the .... method to the fair-value method of accounting for certain assets.

2 .... monitor the banks to make sure that they have enough capital to lend money to customers.

3 The banks' problems emerged as international stock markets started to .... in 2008.

4 The amortised cost accounting system is considered to be particularly useful during a period of ....

5 The specific amount of capital a bank must hold in order to lend a specific amount to customers is known as its ....

6 Under the old system of accounting, banks were forced to .... their assets by very large amounts if asset prices fell.

E **Understanding expressions**

Choose the best explanation for each phrase from the article.

1 '... *relaxing* of fair-value accounting' (article title)
   a) making stricter   b) making easier

2 '... over the lifetime of the *financial instrument*.' (lines 25–26)
   a) an investment such as a bond or share   b) an order to buy shares

3 '... a move that would effectively "*cement*" the use ...' (lines 36–37)
   a) stick   b) formalise

4 '... in order to create *a level playing field* for the international banking sector ...' (lines 40–41)
   a) a situation where the conditions are equal for everyone
   b) a reduction in the volatility of the market

5 '... forced regulators and executives to *face the problems head on* ...' (lines 52–54)
   a) ignore the problems   b) deal with the problems openly

6 '... that fair-value accounting *was pro-cyclical* ...' (lines 65–66)
   a) followed the economic cycle
   b) moved in the opposite direction to the economic cycle

7 '... by *giving in to political pressure* ...' (lines 85–86)
   a) doing something due to political pressure
   b) putting political pressure on someone

8 '... the IASB had permanently damaged its *credibility*.' (lines 88–89)
   a) the extent to which someone can be believed or trusted
   b) the amount of credit someone is allowed to have

OVER TO YOU

1 Taking into account global economic crises, should politicians have the right to suddenly change the accounting rules laid down by 'the world's top accounting rule-making body'? Do you think this episode damaged the International Accounting Standards Board's credibility? Explain your ideas in a short report.

2 Do an Internet search to research further developments in the banking accounting rules or any subsequent banking and accounting crises.

Overseas investment

This unit looks at corporate investment into and out of China.

BEFORE YOU READ

Discuss these questions.

1   Why are global companies keen to expand to China? Do you know any companies which have opened subsidiaries in China? Which industrial sectors do they operate in?

2   Make a list of reasons why Chinese companies might be keen to invest in Western companies.

READING

A   **Understanding the main points**

Read the article on the opposite page and answer these questions.

1   Over the past few years, which three main factors have driven the increase in global corporate investment in China?

2   Which industrial sectors have been particularly open to outside investors?

3   More recently in China, which type of investment has become more common – inward or outward?

4   What are the three main things that China has acquired through overseas mergers and acquisitions?

5   What sort of difficulties has China sometimes encountered in its attempts to buy up overseas companies?

6   Which global business sector is most likely to benefit from investment opportunities in China in the near future?

7   In this article, what do the terms *inbound*, *outbound* and *domestic* refer to?

B   **Understanding details**

Read the article again and say whether these statements are true (T) or false (F). Correct the false ones. Identify the part of the article that gives this information.

1   The next major wave of Chinese mergers and acquisition activity will be internal.

2   Many Chinese retail firms are too small to be interesting to overseas firms, from an investment perspective.

3   China has tried to control its manufacturing costs through outbound acquisition.

4   China's overseas investment will only be made by state-funded firms in the future.

5   Overseas investment by Chinese firms is likely to involve moving production sites to China in order to reduce costs.

6   China is low on financial reserves.

7   A few years ago, Chinese banks had very little spare cash.

8   Overseas banks have provided China with risk-management expertise in the past.

China: Desperate rush for the entrance

by Rod Newing

A Corporate financiers are viewing China as one of the next big investment opportunities. Over the past few years, regulatory reform, economic growth
5 and the opening up of China, following its entry into the World Trade Organisation, have opened up fresh areas for overseas investors, including the financial services sector. China has become
10 a key arena for global investment banks, keen to advise dynamic Chinese companies on mainland expansion opportunities.

B A few years ago, regulatory barriers
15 to foreign investment started to come down in sectors such as chemicals and automotive parts. This led to some inbound mergers and acquisitions (M&A) activity by
20 foreign multinationals.

C More recently, however, the investment banking trend started to focus on advising Chinese companies on their overseas mergers and acquisitions
25 strategy rather than on helping foreign companies do inbound M&A deals. There are a number of reasons for this.

D Firstly, many privately owned Chi-
30 nese companies are run by young entrepreneurs who do not want to sell out to foreign investors. They believe they have years in which to develop their business. Secondly, in sectors
35 such as retail, existing Chinese companies are generally very small scale. This tends to make them less attractive to large foreign multinationals, who prefer to grow their Chinese
40 operations organically instead.

E The size and type of outbound M&A deals in those years increased dramatically. China needed to sustain its breakneck economic growth, so it
45 invested heavily in overseas iron ore, steel and coal mines. Foreign acquisitions in other sectors were seen to be strategically important for China – helping it to access skills that could
50 drive reform across many of its state organisations.

F In the future, private Chinese companies are likely to go for global brands, relocating production to lower-
55 cost mainland factories, as Lenovo did in 2004 when it acquired IBM's personal computing business. Outbound M&A does face its own challenges, however. In June 2005, for example,
60 an $18.5bn hostile bid for Unocal of the US by CNOOC, the state-backed energy giant, failed due to national security concerns in Washington.

G Today, China has a high level of
65 liquidity and can afford to be choosy about who it allows in and which sectors they can play in, whereas several years ago, Chinese lenders were largely broke. At that time,
70 Beijing permitted foreign investors to spend a combined $20bn to acquire stakes in domestic lenders in return for help to improve risk management. More recently, however, it rejected
75 investment offers from a US equity fund and signalled that it was more interested in the banking sector, which offers skills desperately needed by Chinese banks.

H David Chin, a managing director of UBS's investment bank, says: 'Foreign investors want to buy stakes in Chinese lenders, while Chinese banks want to expand with overseas acquisitions.'
85 Foreign investment banks are seeking to acquire stakes in domestic securities firms, in order to be able to underwrite and trade local stocks.

I What next? The Chinese M&A mar-
90 ket has entered a new stage. At first, it was mainly inbound, while outbound activity started to gather pace a few years afterwards. Now, domestic M&A has woken up. And the global
95 investment banking community is ready for it.

FT

C **How the text is organised**

What do these words refer to in the article?

1 its (line 6)

2 this (line 28)

3 it (line 56)

4 that (line 69)

5 it (line 74)

6 it (line 91)

VOCABULARY

A Definitions

Match these words from the article (1–6) with their meanings (a–f).

1	broke	a)	without buying other businesses
2	(to grow) organically	b)	bankrupt
3	liquidity	c)	size
4	breakneck	d)	bank
5	lender	e)	cash
6	scale	f)	extremely fast

B Word partnerships

Match these words to make word partnerships from the article.

1	corporate	a)	investment
2	investment	b)	brands
3	regulatory	c)	management
4	economic	d)	financiers
5	financial	e)	opportunities
6	foreign	f)	growth
7	global	g)	services
8	hostile	h)	reform
9	risk	i)	bid

C Word search

Find words and phrases in the article which fit these meanings.

1 an entity that advises companies on how they can grow by joining with, or buying other companies (paragraph A)

an i........ b........

2 when one company joins with another company to create a larger company (paragraph B)

a m........

3 when one company buys another company or part of another company (paragraph B)

an a........

4 when a foreign company buys a company in your country (paragraph B)

an i........ acquisition

5 somebody who has set up and runs their own company (paragraph D)

an e........

6 when a company in your country takes over a company in a foreign country (paragraph E)

an o........ acquisition

D **Sentence completion**

Use words and phrases from Exercises A–C to complete these sentences.

1   China has become very active in the area of .... and .... in the last few years.

2   China is keen to acquire .... It can reduce costs by moving their manufacturing sites to China.

3   .... are excited about their future prospects in China.

4   In the past, ...-........ expertise was an important by-product of inward investment by foreign financial institutions.

5   .... has resulted in a gradual reduction in regulatory barriers to inward investment into China.

6   This has allowed the amount of .... in China to grow over the last decade.

7   Some Chinese companies are too small .... to be interesting acquisition targets for large foreign multinationals.

8   These days, Chinese banks have plenty of money, but a few years ago, many of them were nearly ....

9   Unocal in the USA was the subject of an unsuccessful .... in 2005.

E **Prepositions**

Complete these phrases using the prepositions in the box.

for   in   in   on   out   to   to   up

1   to open .... fresh areas .... overseas investors

2   to invest heavily .... overseas iron ore, steel and coal mines

3   to relocate production .... lower-cost mainland factories

4   to advise Chinese companies .... their overseas mergers and acquisitions

5   to acquire stakes .... domestic lenders

6   to sell .... foreign investors

OVER TO YOU

1   Do an Internet search to find out about companies which have expanded to China or been completely or partially taken over by a Chinese firm. Write a short summary.

2   Some multinational companies have opened subsidiaries in China through joint ventures with Chinese companies. Write a short report on the potential advantages and disadvantages of doing this.

3   In recent years, China has used its foreign reserves to buy stakes in, or entire, foreign brands. What benefits or risks can foreign ownership pose to a company or country? Outline your ideas in a short presentation.

Start-up capital

This unit looks at new companies which are seeking finance from investors.

Discuss this question.

A completely new company is often referred to as a 'start-up'. In what ways can start-ups be risky ventures? Can you think of any start-ups which have become very successful in the last few years? What factors do you think contributed to their success?

READING

A **Understanding the main points**

Read the article on the opposite page and choose the best option to complete each statement.

1 The problem for most entrepreneurs is that they don't have enough …

   a) ideas.   b) money.   c) time.

2 The riskiest type of company is …

   a) an established company.

   b) a start-up.

   c) a management buyout of part of a large existing company.

3 The main thing that an investor looks for is a start-up company which …

   a) has an interesting product or service.

   b) will pay them back within the first year.

   c) will survive and make a healthy profit.

4 The IRR (internal rate of return) …

   a) indicates how risky the investment could be.

   b) shows how profitable the investment is expected to be.

   c) shows how popular the product or service will be.

B **How the text is organised**

Decide which of these statements best describes the main idea in each paragraph.

1 Whilst experienced investors do not rely totally on a projected IRR, it is an important factor in their investment decision-making.

2 It is much easier to attract investment funding for a well-established business than for a start-up.

3 The majority of start-up companies do not succeed, so an entrepreneur must show potential investors that they can minimise the risk of failure.

4 IRR is a very important part of investment decision-making.

5 New companies which have already started selling their product are still risky investments, but more likely to attract investment capital than a start-up.

Raising funds for schemes and dreams

by Doug Richard

A Companies require capital. Start-up companies – especially high-risk, high-reward, innovation-based companies – frequently need more capital than a start-up entrepreneur can provide. This means that the entrepreneur generally has to look for outside finance. Debt finance, such as a bank loan, is generally much more readily available for the purchase of an existing company or for the management buyout of part of a large, existing company than it is for a start-up, however. Essentially, the risk of these types of transactions is lower because the business in question already exists, and its trading history can be analysed.

B After this, another category of capital is available for innovation companies that have actually established themselves. This is due to the fact that although they have not yet hit the fast-growth curve, they have managed to reduce risk in a variety of ways. Firstly, they have already built a product or service, thereby reducing technical risk. Secondly, they have made some sales, diminishing market risk. Thirdly, an existing effective management team lowers people risk. Although these companies are still put in the high-risk category, they present an attractive balance of risk and reward from the investor's point of view.

C Lack of available investment capital for start-ups, or 'start-up capital', however, means that the success of a start-up depends on how well an entrepreneur's business plan takes into account the needs of a potential investor. Investors need a healthy return on their capital investment. The return they ask for mainly depends on the amount of risk the investment presents: the greater the risk, the greater the required reward. They usually measure return using a calculation known as IRR (internal rate of return). This shows the return in terms of the annual percentage of return the investor is likely to get over the lifetime of the investment. In simplified terms, an IRR of 60 per cent means investors receive back the amount of the original capital plus 60 per cent of the capital for each year of the investment.

D It is also important to remember that investors are usually building a portfolio of investments, which they view as a group. They know that most of the companies will fail completely, some will succeed, but only a few will be very successful. So every company in a portfolio needs to give a potentially high return, because the winners will eventually have to cover the losers. Therefore, the only way for entrepreneurs to interest investors is to demonstrate that they understand the risk factors, and to present a persuasive business plan, with whatever data they can find, to show that the risk will diminish.

E However, smart investors do not rely solely on an IRR calculation because it can be misleading. This is because most of the variables upon which IRR depends are hard to know in the early stages of investment – particularly how long the investment will last and what the selling price will be. Nevertheless, while smart investors may not entirely depend on it, smart entrepreneurs will ensure that their proposition shows the potential for an IRR of the magnitude that investors like to see before taking the big step of investing in a start-up company.

FT

C **Understanding details**

Read the article again and say whether these statements are true (T) or false (F). Correct the false ones. Identify the part of the article that gives this information.

1 Banks tend to prefer to lend money to low-risk companies.

2 It is easier for potential investors to make investment decisions about a business which is already running.

3 Innovation companies which have actually built a product or service are considered to be low-risk investments.

4 Investors in start-up companies will not invest in risky ventures, however profitable they might potentially be.

5 The IRR shows the rate of return on the investment for the first year.

6 Start-up investors expect all their investments to succeed.

VOCABULARY

A **Word partnerships**

Complete these word partnerships with words from the article. Use the definitions to help you.

1 **start-up** a) ....   type of enterprise that finds it more difficult to find outside financiers
   start-up b) ....   person who sets up a new company
   start-up c) ....   finance for a newly set-up company

2 a) .... **risk**   if the managers running the company do not have the right experience or ideas
   b) .... **risk**   if there is a fault with a new product or it does not do what it says it will do
   c) .... **risk**   if the product does not sell because either it is not in demand or there are too many other competing products already on sale

3 a) d........ f........
   b) i........ c........   two types of money that start-up entrepreneurs need

B **Word search**

Find phrases in the article which complete these sentences.

1 Projects which promise a high rate of return are often also h........-r........ projects, likely to fail in the early stages. (paragraph A)

2 When the managers of a company decide to break away from that company and buy part of it in order to run it separately, it is known as a m........ b......... (paragraph A)

3 When the sales of start-up companies start to rise quickly, this is known as hitting a f........-g........ curve. (paragraph B).

4 A company which develops a new product or service is known as an i........ c......... (paragraph B)

5 The i........ r........ of r........ is the figure most commonly used by investors to judge whether a potential investment is a good idea or not. (paragraph C)

6 Potential investors need to study and have confidence in a start-up company's b........ p........ before they will take the risk of investing in it. (paragraph D)

7 When investors invest in a range of companies, they are said to have a p........ of i......... (paragraph D)

8 Investors are only prepared to take the high risks associated with investing in start-ups if they are likely to generate a h........ r......... (paragraph D)

C **Text completion**

Use the words in the box to complete the paragraph.

fail   fund   investor   IRR   return   venture   worth

Some simple arithmetic illustrates the investor's decision-making process. Let us say an ....[1] intends to invest £1m into each of 10 companies for five years. The investor requires a ....[2] equal to the average return for early stage investors in ....[3] capital in the US, which is an ....[4] above 20 per cent. That means his total ....[5] must double in size in five years. Assuming six of the 10 companies ....[6] and two companies achieve a 20-per-cent IRR, the other two must each return an IRR of 140 per cent. In other words, they must be ....[7] £8m in five years. That is extremely fast growth!

D Understanding expressions

Choose the best explanation for each phrase from the article.

1 'Investors need a *healthy return* on their capital investment.' (lines 41–42)

  a) large return   b) safe return

2 '... the winners will eventually have to *cover* the losers.' (lines 65–66)

  a) be more numerous than   b) financially compensate the investor for

3 '... it can be *misleading*.' (lines 75–76)

  a) inaccurate   b) highly accurate

4 '... most of the *variables* upon which ...' (line 77)

  a) individual factors   b) changeable amounts

5 '... an IRR of the *magnitude* that investors like to see ...' (lines 85–86)

  a) size   b) magnificence

E Sentence completion

Use expressions from Exercises A–D to complete these sentences.

1 Last year, we added three more ....-........ companies to our portfolio of ....

2 We think that one of the companies looks particularly promising. It claims a very high .... of ....

3 This is good, because obviously this company might well have to .... the other two companies if they fail, as so many start-ups do in their first year of trading.

4 All of the ....-........ .... tried to persuade us that they would all provide a return of the .... we were looking for.

5 However, we particularly liked the .... of one of the three companies, which we finally decided to give .... capital to.

6 We expect to see their sales hit the ....-........ .... very soon.

7 If they succeed, the companies will be .... much more to future investors.

8 All we ask from these investments is a ....!

1 Type the word *start-up* into your Internet search engine. Find out about one or two newly set-up companies, or people who provide money or advice on how to succeed with a start-up company. Write a short report.

2 Imagine a new product (or product range) or service which you think would be a guaranteed success as a start-up company. Make a short presentation or 'pitch' to a panel of start-up venture capitalists. Explain your product or service, which market it would be aimed at, how much money you would need and what rate of return you would expect to make over the next five years.

Options trading

This unit looks at the risks and rewards of trading in share options in Porsche's attempted takeover of Volkswagen.

BEFORE YOU READ

Discuss these questions.

1   We generally assume that a company's success depends on what it does in its core business market. Can you think of any other activities which can make money for a company?

2   Explain what you know about the Porsche brand and its business history.

3   The title of the article is a pun. Which famous personality's name does it refer to? Remove three letters from the first word to get that name. Why do you think the author associated this personality with the Porsche brand?

READING

A   Understanding the main points

Read the article on the opposite page and say whether these statements are true (T) or false (F). Correct the false ones. Identify the part of the article that gives this information.

At the time this performance report was written (February 2009), ...

1   the luxury car market was doing very well.

2   Porsche's financial trading strategies were not at all risky.

3   the gradual takeover of Volkswagen by Porsche had helped to make Porsche a lot of money.

4   Porsche was making more money from financial operations than it was from selling cars.

5   Porsche would have no difficulty buying up the rest of the VW shares.

6   there was a clear risk that VW's share price could fall in the future.

7   HSBC agreed with Porsche's valuation of its VW shares.

B   Understanding details

Read the article again and answer these questions.

1   Which other German groups were in danger due to share trading activities?

2   How much profit did Porsche make in 2008 from trading options?

3   How much profit did Porsche make from its core activities in that year?

4   What percentage of VW shares did Porsche hope to have acquired in the near future?

5   Who was standing in the way of a full takeover? How large was their stake in VW?

6   How was Porsche trying to solve that problem?

7   How much cash did VW hold, and how could Porsche use this if it was successful in taking over VW?

Porsche spice

A Daimler's very poor results yesterday show that even luxury car makers are running out of fuel. So investors in its high-speed counterpart, Porsche, must be very pleased to hear that it generated €400m liquidity last year from trading options on German companies. Its financial engineering skills, it would seem, match its automotive ones.

B But this way lies danger. Fellow German groups Schaeffler and Merckle risk losing control of their business empires due to the fact that they made some highly leveraged share acquisitions and then saw a collapse in the value of shares, which had been used as collateral against the loans for these shares.

C Porsche's slowly-slowly takeover of Volkswagen (VW), via cash-settled call options, has so far proved extremely profitable. The short squeeze (much higher demand than supply) on VW shares dramatically pushed up its share price, when Porsche revealed its full position in October 2008. This helped it make a cool €6.8bn profit from options trades in that year, whereas it made only €1bn from selling cars. Porsche easily took over 50 per cent of VW in January 2009.

D There is an uncertain road ahead, however. Porsche probably has enough remaining options to get close to its next target: 75 per cent of VW. It also hopes that a German law, which currently allows the State of Lower Saxony to exercise a blocking minority via its 20-per-cent stake in VW, will be changed by a legal challenge to the European Commission.

E If it is successful, Porsche could take over the rest of VW, part-financed by VW's €10bn cash pile. However, the European case could go the wrong way. While Porsche says that it does not need a law change to buy up to 75 per cent of VW's shares, there seems little point in buying up to 75 per cent without it.

F Since counterparties have hedged their exposure by buying up VW shares, for the moment, these VW options are creating a share shortage. This has boosted the share price to a sky-high €240.

G If the European Commission legal challenge were unsuccessful, and Porsche decided not to buy the remaining amount of shares to take its stake to 75 per cent, so closed its options position, VW's free float would increase, and the price of its shares would consequently fall. What would happen then?

H Porsche says it values VW at €117 a share in its books. Hong Kong Shanghai Banking Corporation (HSBC), however, estimates fair value of VW's shares at a much more conservative €74, on a sum-of-the-parts basis. The bank says that this reflects VW's superior outlook compared to that of many of its competitors. What is more, if you multiply the 2010 earnings per share of €6.45 by ten times – which is a common way to estimate the real value of shares – the result is even lower.

I Therefore, should Porsche fail in its European Commission challenge and consequently have to write down its VW stake, investors will wish it had stuck to building sports cars, not derivatives positions.

FT

VOCABULARY

A **Word search**

Find words or phrases in the article which fit these meanings.

1 the use of various mathematical tools to maximise profits from financial investments (paragraph A)

f........e........

2 when the major part of an investment is funded by borrowed money (paragraph B)

h........l........

3 assets which are promised by a borrower to a lender if the borrower cannot repay a loan (also known as *security*) (paragraph B)

c........

4 when (for example) shares that are bought on a financial market are paid for with real money (paragraph C)

c........-s........

5 the number of shares in a company needed to veto certain decisions at the Annual General Meeting of shareholders (paragraph D)

b........m........

6 the amount of money an investor risks losing if the investment does badly, for example on the stock market (paragraph F)

e........

7 when there are not enough shares available on the market to supply the demand for them

a) s........s........ (paragraph C)
b) s........s........ (paragraph F)

8 when the number of shares in supply exceed the number which are in demand, this amount of shares are said to be the company's f........f........ of shares. (paragraph G)

B **Vocabulary development**

Match these words and phrases (1–6) with their meanings (a–f).

1	derivatives	a)	the right to buy or sell shares, bonds, currencies or commodities at a particular price within a particular period of time or on a particular date in the future
2	option	b)	the right to sell shares at a specific price in the future, which you buy because you think prices will fall below that price
3	option trade	c)	the buying or selling of an option
4	call option	d)	sell an option back at the current market price, or let it expire in order to reverse the original transaction or to exit the trade
5	put option	e)	options or futures belong to this group of instruments which often offer investors an easy way to make bets in markets that would otherwise be difficult to get access to
6	to close an option position	f)	the right to buy shares at a specific price in the future because you think that the market price will rise above that price

C **Word partnerships**

Match the verbs (1–6) with the phrases (a–f). Then match each combination with a definition (i–vi).

1	generate	a)	as collateral	i)	to make cash
2	pledge	b)	exposure	ii)	to publicly declare the number of shares you own in a company
3	reveal	c)	its stake	iii)	when a small (but significant enough) shareholder uses its voting rights to veto a proposal at a company's AGM
4	exercise	d)	its position	iv)	to reduce its value on the balance sheet
5	hedge	e)	liquidity	v)	to use as security against a debt
6	write down	f)	a blocking minority	vi)	to protect against financial risk

D **Sentence completion**

Use words and phrases from Exercises A–C to complete these sentences.

1 Porsche had been making a larger profit out of .... trading than it has out of selling cars.

2 Little by little, it had bought up a large percentage of VW share ....

3 The outcome of Porsche's European Commission challenge to the State of Lower Saxony's .... of 20% would decide whether they continued to do this.

4 Up to now, the demand for VW shares had been higher than supply. This .... (or ....) had kept their price very high.

5 However, if Porsche did not win its European court case, it would probably decide not to take its stake to 75%, and would .... its options .... on the remaining VW shares. If it didn't continue buying the shares, their .... would increase significantly.

6 If this happened, the share price would go down and Porsche would have to .... them ....

7 In this case, Porsche might wish that it had focused only on its core skills and had not entered into the world of ....

OVER TO YOU

1 What are the advantages and disadvantages of companies engaging heavily in stock-market trading as well as carrying out their normal business? Think of market conditions, unexpected economic and financial events and the company's investors. Explain your ideas.

2 The article in this unit describes the set of circumstances in 2008 and early 2009. Do an Internet search to find out what has happened to both companies in the meantime. Did Porsche win its European Commission challenge over the German state of Lower Saxony's right to exercise a blocking minority? Did it succeed in taking over VW completely? What is VW's share price valued at today? Write a short report.

This unit looks at the way in which the internal information that companies collect, use and report is changing.

Discuss these questions.

1   What sort of information have companies traditionally published in their annual reports?
2   Can you think of any other information which might be of interest to the investor, the customer or the wider community?
3   There is a pun in the title. Which two words can be combined to form an informal expression which is used to describe accountants?
4   Which type of issues do you think the phrase *green beans* refers to?

A   Understanding the main points

Read the article on the opposite page and answer these questions.

1   Why didn't company accountants generally report on environmental or social issues in the past?
2   Which fundamental change did Mark Bromley, Head of Business Performance at EDF, want to bring about in the company?
3   Which external project did he participate in?
4   Which financial tool did the Prince of Wales's project create to help businesses with their financial reporting?
5   What is the main aim of this tool?
6   Was Aviva CSR Director Louella Eastman's trialling of this tool a success or a failure?
7   At Aviva, what two positive changes resulted from the trial?
8   What is the best way to make company directors take notice of sustainability issues?

B   Understanding details

Read the article again and answer these questions.

1   Which environmental goal did EDF set in 2006?
2   At Aviva, which department did the CSR department work with to collect environmental data?
3   Which five environmental factors did Aviva monitor?
4   Is the interest in sustainability issues limited to the private sector?
5   Which two external groups are encouraging companies to pay attention to sustainability issues?

Counters face up to green beans

by **Robert Bruce**

A When it comes to taking action on climate change, few outsiders would view accountancy as being a green profession. A few years ago, that would have been true. Finance directors did not consider environmental or social factors, except for rare cases such as the Exxon Valdez oil-spill disaster, in their annual reports.

B But times are changing. The reason is simple: figures. If accountants have figures to measure, then they can see how environmental issues affect an organisation's overall strategy.

C In 2006, EDF Energy set up a Sustainable Future project using corporate social responsibility (CSR) as a business performance driver. They wanted to radically transform their business culture, and set a target to reduce carbon emissions from their energy generation activities by 60 per cent by 2020.

D Mark Bromley, Head of Business Performance at EDF Energy, became involved in the work of the Prince of Wales's Accounting for Sustainability Project. He wanted to find an effective reporting system for the company. So he started trialling the connected reporting framework, which the project had devised and promoted.

E 'This was fully in line with our thinking, and we used it as a dynamic management reporting tool,' he says. The framework aims to ensure that sustainability measures are not isolated in a CSR report but are connected to the main financial reporting system. This way, they can have a direct impact on corporate strategy.

F Louella Eastman, Group CSR Director at insurance group Aviva, pioneered the use of the connected reporting framework within the group, aligning non-financial and financial data. In partnership with the finance function, the CSR team collected information on the five environmental areas outlined in the report: polluting emissions, waste and usage of water, energy and other finite resources. The findings were extremely interesting, and the connection of the two disciplines produced strategic change.

G She says, 'It became a discussion about cost. For example, we moved our cleaners onto a day shift from evenings and told the security staff to switch the lights off.' This was a simple action which brought about serious financial change. It came from connecting the CSR information and personnel with the finance function. It translated into significant savings and, more importantly, moved sustainability onto senior executives' agendas.

H Pharmaceuticals group Astra Zeneca also got rid of its sustainability section in the annual report and put the important information into the main figures. Instead of being an add-on, sustainability has become 'fully embedded' in the normal reporting processes of the business. If you show how it links with strategy, it becomes more fundamental to running the business.

I Sustainability issues are moving up the priority lists of both the private and public sector. Companies now consider being sustainable more of a business priority than just a means of persuading the public that they are doing 'good things'. However, the change is being driven from outside, as well as inside organisations. It has become an important issue when recruiting the best graduates into an organisation, for example. Equally, it has become a key issue with customers, particularly in the retail sector.

J Up to now, however, it has mainly been a question of accountants learning to manage the information and allowing their organisations to see the true strategic effects of sustainability figures.

FT

VOCABULARY

A **Word search**

Find word and phrases in the article which match these meanings.

1 environmentally aware (title)

g........

2 when a company takes into account environmental and social factors (paragraph C)

c........ s........ r........

3 management which respects the environment and the future interests of society (paragraph D)

s........

4 what the Prince of Wales's project tackles (paragraph D)

a........ for s........

5 a structure which supports something (paragraph D)

f........

6 when something has a fundamental influence on an organisation's decision-making (paragraph F)

s........

B **Word families**

Complete the chart.

verb	adjective/participle	noun
.... 1	 2	sustainability
.... 3	measurable/measured	 4
.... 5	 6	transformation
connect	 7	 8
.... 9	isolated	 10
reduce	 11	 12
align	 13	 14
pioneer	 15	 16

C **Word partnerships**

Match the verbs (1–10) with the phrases (a–j) to make expressions similar to ones found in the article.

1 to affect
2 to use CSR
3 to radically transform
4 to find
5 to trial
6 to use the connected reporting framework
7 to connect sustainability
8 to align
9 to produce
10 to become

a) the connected reporting framework
b) to the main reporting system
c) an organisation's strategy
d) your business culture
e) as a dynamic management tool
f) strategic change
g) as a business performance driver
h) non-financial and financial data
i) an effective reporting system
j) fully embedded in the normal reporting processes

D Sentence completion

Use words and phrases from Exercises A–C to complete these sentences.

1 .... is now an important consideration in the corporate board room.

2 This factor is now increasingly being fully .... in companies' normal reporting processes.

3 A company's approach to .... no longer needs to be isolated in a separate report.

4 Companies can use a .... framework to link financial and non-financial data.

5 For some companies, the results of this have had a .... impact on company values and behaviours.

6 In these companies, sustainability has actually become an important business ....

7 One day, maybe even accountancy will be considered a .... profession!

E Synonyms

Find three verbs in paragraphs F and G of the article which have the same meaning as *to result in*. Write them in their infinitive form.

F Understanding expressions

Choose the best explanation for each phrase from the article.

1 '... as a *business performance driver*.' (lines 17–18)

   a) something which measures performance   b) something which improves performance

2 '... *trialling* the connected reporting framework ...' (lines 30–31)

   a) to judge a court case   b) to test a new process

3 'This was *fully in line with our thinking* ...' (lines 33–34)

   a) matched our corporate values   b) gave us some good ideas

4 '... *moved sustainability onto senior executives' agendas*.' (lines 66–67)

   a) put sustainability on top of executives' diaries   b) made executives start to take sustainability seriously

5 'Instead of being *an add-on*, ...' (line 72)

   a) an increase   b) a separate feature

6 '... sustainability has *become "fully embedded" in* the normal ...' (lines 72–74)

   a) been totally integrated   b) become lost in the middle of

OVER TO YOU

1 Do an Internet search for the annual accounts of several well-known companies. Find out whether they report sustainability issues. If so, which particular issues are involved? Are they contained in a separate CSR report, or are they connected to the main financial report? Write a short report.

2 Think of an educational or corporate organisation you know of. Brainstorm a list of measures that it could take to reduce its environmental impact as well as its costs. Give a short presentation.

3 'Companies need clear targets and strategies. Reporting can help drive change, but the big problem is the lack of consistency in reporting, as there are no clear guidelines. We need an international standard.' Do you agree with this statement? Should governments and international accounting bodies introduce formal sustainability reporting rules, or should public- and private-sector organisations decide their own sustainability management and reporting strategies? Discuss your ideas.

Responsible investing

This unit looks at the way in which the criteria that investors use to make investment decisions is changing.

Discuss these questions.

1 When investors are deciding whether to invest in a company or a project, which single factor do they generally consider to be the most important?

2 Do you think an investor should take into account the impact the company or project might also have on the environment or the local community? Explain your ideas.

READING

A **Understanding the main points**

Read the article on the opposite page and answer these questions.

1 Which factors have asset managers traditionally considered when choosing investments?

2 What sort of investment process are they more interested in these days?

3 As well as helping the planet, what aspect of investing does this process improve?

4 How does sustainable investment help to ensure the long-term financial stability of the planet?

5 Which class of assets do many sustainable investments involve?

6 Why is it often easier to persuade investors to invest in sustainable property management than in real-estate?

7 What is Oxford Group's investment philosophy?

8 What concern does the author express about sustainable investment?

B **Understanding details**

Read the article again and answer these questions.

1 Which organisation has produced a guide to the ESG factors relating to companies which are quoted on the stock market?

2 Which other organisations have an interest in responsible investment?

3 In which three ways do investors benefit when dealing with companies with strong sustainability policies?

4 Which environmental consideration was a particular feature of Oxford Group's sustainable property projects in Eastern Europe and Near Asia?

5 Which sort of areas are ideal for sustainable property investment projects, following Oxford Group's example?

6 What sort of supply chain is used in these projects?

Investing in doing good can be good risk management

by Alice Clegg

A Choosing investments by simply looking at a company's financial statements and deciding how the current share price relates to the fair value of the stock is so old-fashioned!

B These days, even the most commercially minded asset managers are talking about a sustainable investment process, including a checklist of corporate responsibility and human rights issues. Many industry participants agree that this is the way forward.

C One significant driver of the increasing interest in ESG (environmental, social and governance) factors is the part they play in improving risk management. People don't want any surprises these days, and an ESG framework helps you manage an aspect of risk.

D 'This isn't a manifesto for saving the planet, it's a tool for better assessing risk,' says Charles Cronin, Head of the Chartered Financial Analyst (CFA) Institute Centre for Financial Market Integrity, Europe, Middle East and Africa (EMEA). 'It's just another way of peeling the investment onion.' The CFA Institute provides at manual for investors on how to identify ESG factors at listed companies, and how to integrate these factors into traditional financial analysis.

E Helena Vines Fiestas, a policy analyst for Oxfam, says, 'Responsible investors benefit from better risk management, greater transparency and an active engagement with companies to promote better management.' ESG issues are key features of their investment analysis. Whilst Oxfam clearly has an agenda, such as reducing third-world poverty, it is engaging with investors who feel that their legal duty to maximise financial returns is far more important than 'doing good'.

F 'If you invest in ways that don't undermine the financial system [by being careful about the long-term impact of your investment behaviour], that's economically rational,' says Colin Melvin, Chief Executive of Hermes Equity Ownership Services. 'That economic rationality has been absent for some time.'

G Although many sustainable investment initiatives involve equities, this is not the only class of assets affected by the new ways of thinking. Real-estate investment is also changing, although environmentally friendly property management is much easier to justify to investors because it involves saving energy, which in turn saves costs.

H Oxford Group invested in sustainable property projects in Eastern Europe and Near Asia, involving renewable energy, which promised to deliver a minimum of 25 per cent per annum over the three-and-a-half-year life of the fund.

I However, that is not the only way for property investment to be sustainable. By investing in areas designated as regeneration targets, integrating developments into local infrastructure (sustainable community building) and using a sustainable supply chain, Hadley Barrett, Oxford Group's CEO, is confident he can meet this goal. 'Even in a falling market, our investment philosophy of adding value to projects, rather than simply engaging in price speculation, creates value for investors.'

J Whether it is about better risk management, a clear conscience, greater financial returns or good PR, more and more asset managers are jumping on the bandwagon. The argument is that growth will have to come from these sectors if the future of humanity is to be secure. Therefore they provide an excellent investment opportunity. Whether being green is really profitable in difficult markets, however, remains to be seen.

FT

C   **How the text is organised**

Find these linking words and phrases in the article. Tick (✓) the ones that are used to express contrast.

1 even (line 6) ☐

2 including (line 9) ☐

3 whilst (line 41) ☐

4 such as (line 42) ☐

5 although (line 56) ☐

6 also (line 60) ☐

7 because (line 63) ☐

8 however (line 72) ☐

9 rather than (line 83) ☐

10 whether (line 85) ☐

VOCABULARY

A **Word search**

1 Find word partnerships containing *investment* in the article which fit these meanings.

1 s........ investment   investment which takes into account environmental, social and governance considerations

2 investment a........   the process of deciding whether an investment would be a good one or not

3 investment b........   the way investors choose their investments

4 r........-e........ investment   investment in property

5 investment o........   a stock which might be good to invest in

2 Find phrases in the article which fit these meanings.

1 the people who are responsible for investing in equities on behalf of their clients (paragraph B)

     a........ m........

2 the process by which investment managers try to reduce the potential risks of investing in a particular asset (paragraph C)   r........m........

3 a system which companies use to assess the environmental and social impact of their investments (paragraph C)   ESG f........

4 a company which is registered on a stock exchange so that its stocks can be publicly traded on the stock market (paragraph D)   l........ company

5 the use of this in a property is a way of being environmentally responsible (paragraph H)

     r........ e........

6 responsible investors aim to do this to projects, rather than just make a quick profit (paragraph I)

     a........ v........ to projects

7 a negative investment strategy employed by irresponsible investors (paragraph I)

     p........ s........

B **Word partnerships**

Match the verbs (1–10) with the phrases (a–j) to make expressions similar to those in the article.

1 to assess	a) world poverty
2 to integrate ESG factors	b) long-term impact of investment behaviour
3 to reduce	c) risk
4 to maximise	d) into local infrastructure
5 to be careful about the	e) sustainable property projects
6 to integrate developments	f) into traditional financial analysis
7 to invest in	g) financial returns
8 to use a sustainable	h) price speculation
9 to add	i) value to projects
10 to engage in	j) supply chain

C Sentence completion

Use words and phrases from Exercises A and B in the correct form to complete these sentences.

1 Responsible asset managers can use an ESG .... to help them choose sustainable investments.

2 Taking ESG factors into account can help investors with the .... of their investments.

3 You can check the level of corporate responsibility of .... companies in a guide produced by the CFA Institute.

4 A different class of investment asset to equities, involving property, is ....

5 Investment policies based simply on .... are unlikely to take ESG factors into account.

6 Responsible investors look at more than just a company's financial statements when engaging in .... to decide what to invest in.

7 They want to .... more than simply financial .... to an investment.

8 They can do this by using a .... chain to source their materials.

D Understanding expressions

Choose the best explanation for each phrase from the article.

1 'One *significant driver* of the increasing interest in [...] ESG factors ...' (lines 13–15)
   a) major motivating force
   b) important leader

2 'This isn't a *manifesto* for saving the planet, ...' (lines 21–22)
   a) a political argument
   b) an official list of goods being carried on a ship or aircraft

3 'It's just another way of *peeling the investment onion*.' (lines 27–28)
   a) making an investment
   b) analysing an investment opportunity

4 'Whilst Oxfam clearly has *an agenda*, ...' (lines 41–42)
   a) a busy diary
   b) specific issues it wishes to fight for

5 '... ways that don't *undermine the financial system* ...' (lines 47–48)
   a) cause an economic downturn or breakdown
   b) support the financial system

6 '... that's *economically rational* ...' (line 51)
   a) good value for money
   b) makes good economic sense

7 '... more and more asset managers are *jumping on the bandwagon*.' (lines 87–89)
   a) starting to follow the same practices
   b) exercising better judgement

8 'Whether *being green* is ...' (lines 94)
   a) being naive
   b) considering the environment

OVER TO YOU

1 Can you think of any companies which publicise the fact that they have environmental and social responsibility on their agenda? Do you think this makes them more attractive to investors, or do you think that quick profits will always be an investor's main priority? Explain your reasons.

2 Choose several well-known multinational companies and look them up on the Internet. Check what they say about their ESG policy in the annual report. Write a short summary.

Corporate governance

This unit looks at a corporate scandal involving the chairman of a listed company.

Discuss these questions.

1   In the past, a number of large and well-known companies, such as Enron, Parmelat and Worldcom, became the subject of high-profile corporate scandals. Explain what you know about these scandals or similar ones that you know of.

2   What sort of effect can a corporate scandal have on the business environment? Think about the company's employees and business partners, suppliers and customers, the industry it operates in, accounting and finance firms and the stock market, as well as their rules and regulators.

A   Understanding the main points

Read the article on the opposite page and say whether these statements are true (T) or false (F). Correct the false ones. Identify the part of the article that gives this information.

1   The crime was committed in China.

2   It concerned one of the country's largest, most well-respected companies.

3   The Chairman stole money from the company.

4   The company's auditors and stock-market regulators had warned everyone of the corporate fraud that was taking place at Satyam.

5   The Chairman used his family's shares in Maytas as security to people who had lent money to the company.

6   He had told the other shareholders who these shares now technically belonged to.

7   The new shareholders sold their shares, which resulted in a share price crash.

8   This case resulted in stricter disclosure rules for controlling shareholders of Indian companies.

B   How the text is organised

> Certain phrases can be used to introduce the reason why something happened (cause) or what happened as a consequence of certain actions (effect).

Decide whether these phrases are used to introduce a cause or an effect in the article.

1   ... *as a result*, the company's share price had plummeted ... (lines 62–63)

2   *In response to* the fraud, the corporate community called for ... (lines 65–66)

3   This is *due to the fact that* ... (line 74)

4   ... it will *trigger* a margin call ... (lines 76–77)

5   *Consequently*, the stock price can collapse. (lines 77–78)

Scandal raises questions about disclosure rules

by Joe Leahy

A In early 2009, B. Ramalinga Raju, the Chairman of Satyam Computer Services, India's fourth-largest information technology group by revenue, shocked
5 India and the rest of the corporate world. In a letter to his Board of Directors, he confessed to a crime so spectacular in its scale that many could hardly believe it. 'Dear Board Mem-
10 bers, It is with deep regret … that I would like to bring the following facts to your notice …'

B It seemed that everything, from revenue and profits to most of Satyam's
15 cash balance of Rs53.61bn ($1.1bn) on its balance sheet as of September 2008, was an invention. In one step, he had undermined the confidence of India's normally self-assured busi-
20 ness community.

C Shockingly, this fraud had occurred in a multi-billion-dollar information technology outsourcing business in what was regarded as one of the most-
25 progressive industries in India's corporate sector. Symbolically, it was similar to the high-profile financial scandals at Enron, Worldcom or Parmalat, all of which had overstated profits and the
30 value of assets on their books.

D Furthermore, the scam had, it appeared, been carried out over a number of years, which raised questions over just how the company's auditor,
35 PwC, and stock-market regulators had failed to spot it. India's troubled stock market felt the negative effects of the revelations. On the day of the confession alone, the Mumbai Stock
40 Exchange's benchmark Sensex Index went down by 7.24 per cent.

E The episode began when, on December 16, Mr Raju suddenly proposed that Satyam acquire his family's May-
45 tas property and infrastructure companies in a deal worth $1.6bn. Satyam's independent directors approved the deal, but within hours Mr Raju was forced to abandon the plan after institu-
50 tional investors rejected it.

F What these investors didn't know was that Mr Raju was sitting on a time bomb. He had pledged his family's 8-per-cent stake in Satyam to lenders.
55 These lenders had, in turn, started selling off the shares as Satyam's stock fell in line with the rest of the stock market. The Maytas deal was, in fact, an attempt to cover up the fraud at Satyam.

G By January 7, the game was up. The lenders had sold almost all of the Raju family's shares and, as a result, the company's share price had plummeted to a fraction of its former value.

H In response to the fraud, the corporate community called for the government to make corporate disclosure requirements stricter. The most obvious need was to force controlling
70 shareholders to reveal if they had pledged their shares in their companies to lenders, a key risk for minority investors who might be unaware of this fact. This is due to the fact that once a
75 stock that has been pledged drops to a certain price, it will trigger a margin call, forcing the sale of that share. Consequently, the stock price can collapse.

I In a market in which more than half
80 of the key companies listed on the Sensex are controlled by families, disclosure was a sensitive issue, however. Nevertheless, two weeks after the confession, the Securities and
85 Exchange Board of India (SEBI), the stock-market regulator, made it mandatory for controlling shareholders to declare their share pledges. The move was welcomed by the market, but
90 experts described it as 'too little, too late'.

FT

Understanding details

Read the article again and answer these questions.

1 Which business sector was Satyam in?

2 What is the name of the most famous Mumbai stock-market index?

3 Why did Mr Raju ask Satyam to buy his family business, Maytas?

4 What is a common feature of many of India's top companies?

5 Which financial authority introduced a law which forced controlling shareholders to openly declare any company shares pledged to other people?

VOCABULARY

A Word search

Find words or phrases in the article which fit these meanings.

1 the position that B. Ramalinga Raju held with Satyam Computer Services (paragraph A) *C*........

2 the group of a company's executives (paragraph A) *B*........ of *D*........

3 a synonym for *fraud* (paragraph D) *s*........

4 directors who do not represent a large institution (paragraph E) *i*........ *d*........

5 large companies which invest heavily in something (paragraph E) *i*........ *i*........

6 people who own more than half of the shares in a company (paragraph H) *c*........ *s*........

7 people who own a small number of shares in a company (paragraph H) *m*........ *i*........

8 when a company has to to publish information about its financial activities by law for the benefit of investors (paragraph H) *c*........ *d*........ *r*........

9 the role that SEBI, for instance, plays in the financial markets (paragraph I)
   s........-*m*........ *r*........

B Vocabulary development

1 Put these words and phrases into the correct column.

1 fall	4 rocket	7 rise	10 remain constant	13 drop
2 plummet	5 increase	8 crash	11 climb	14 remain stable
3 remain steady	6 flatten out	9 soar	12 dive	15 jump

A upward movement	B downward movement	C level (no movement)

2 Complete this paragraph, which explains the process of share pledging, using the words in the box.

| borrow   lender   pledge   security |

When shareholders wish to ....[1] money, they can use their shares as ....[2] against the loan. So they ....[3] them to the person who is lending them the capital. If they are unable to repay the loan, the ....[4] has the right to take these shares and sell them.

3 Complete this paragraph, which describes why and how a 'margin call' is triggered, using the phrases in the box.

| margin call   minimum margin   on margin   share broker |

When an investor buys more shares than the value of their capital will pay for, they take out a loan from the ....[1]. In return, this agent requires a ....[2], or percentage of the total value of the shares, to be funded by the investor's capital or equity at all times. This is known as buying shares ....[3]. During a poor period of trading, if the value of the shares drops sufficiently that the value of the equity part no longer covers that margin, the broker will put out a ....[4]. As a result, the investor may need to sell some of their shares in order to raise the additional funds to meet the required margin on their remaining investments.

C Sentence completion

Use words and phrases from Reading Exercise B and Vocabulary Exercises A and B
to complete these sentences.

1 Mr Raju, the Chairman of Satyam Computer Services, must have been very ashamed when he
confessed his crime to his .... of ....

2 India's ....-........ ...., the SEBI, failed to spot the fraud for many years.

3 .... a .... of the fraud, it imposed new .... requirements for controlling shareholders.

4 .... are better protected by the new disclosure requirements in India.

5 They now know when a major shareholder has .... shares as .... against a loan.

6 In falling stock-market conditions, when share prices can ...., an automatic ....
will force shareholders to sell their shares.

D Understanding expressions

Choose the best explanation for each phrase from the article.

1 '... a crime so *spectacular in its scale* ...' (lines 7–8)

   a) very large   b) exciting

2 *It is with deep regret* ... that ...' (line 10)

   a) I am very happy to   b) I am very sorry to

3 '... to *bring the following facts to your notice* ...' (lines 11–12)

   a) inform you about   b) put a notice up

4 '... had *undermined the confidence of* ...' (line 18)

   a) caused them to lose confidence   b) exposed their confidence

5 '... normally *self-assured* business community.' (lines 19–20)

   a) heavily insured   b) self-confident

6 '... one of the most *progressive* industries ...' (lines 24–25)

   a) growing fast   b) modern in its behaviour

7 '... the Mumbai Stock Exchange's *benchmark* Sensex Index ...' (lines 39–40)

   a) by which the general trend can be measured   b) most well known

8 '... *the game was up*.' (line 60)

   a) the fraud couldn't be concealed any longer   b) the company had closed

---

OVER TO YOU

1 Do an online search to find out the latest developments in India's largest corporate fraud, which has
been dubbed 'India's Enron'. What has happened to Satyam in the meantime? Has the investigation
been completed and a verdict reached on those who were alleged to have been involved in the cover-
up? Write a short report, outlining the findings to date.

2 Do an online search of a corporate fraud which interests you. Write a short summary.

Investment credit rating

This unit looks at the role of the corporate credit-rating agencies in the global economic crisis which started in 2007.

Discuss these questions.

1 If you wanted to borrow money, what would the lender do to assure themselves that you would be able to pay it back in the future?
2 If you were going to make an investment in a company or financial product, how would you check whether your investment would be safe?

READING

A **Understanding the main points**

Read the article and say whether these statements are true (T) or false (F).
Correct the false ones. Identify the part of the article that gives this information.

1 At the time of its failure, Northern Rock was a building society.
2 It provided money for borrowers to buy homes and property.
3 It suddenly experienced financing problems and had to ask the Bank of England for help.
4 Northern Rock's customers feared they would lose their savings and started taking them out of the bank quickly.
5 The UK government blamed only Northern Rock for this crisis.
6 Corporate credit agencies advise investors on the riskiness of companies and investment products.
7 Standard & Poor credit-rating agency admitted that it had never warned the investor community of the danger of these 'securitisation' products.

B **Understanding details**

Read the article again and answer these questions.

1 Over which period did Northern Rock increase in size very quickly?
2 Which particular financial problem made it difficult for Northern Rock to find money to finance its lending activities?
3 Which three credit-rating agencies dominated the world market at that time?
4 Which rating do they give to the safest investments?
5 Which rating do they give to the riskiest investments?
6 Who pays the credit agencies for their work?
7 What was Jean-Claude Trichet's opinion about the number of credit agencies in the market?
8 Which organisation decided to investigate and improve the credit-agency sector?

A The Northern Rock Building Society converted into a public limited company in 1997. Over the next 10 years, the Northern Rock Bank rapidly grew into one of the largest mortgage lenders in the UK, relying on a system of securitisation – repackaging most of the loans it had originated into securities and selling them on to institutional investors.

B In 2007, the US subprime crisis hit Europe. That source of financing dried up, so the bank was forced to borrow emergency money from the Bank of England. When customers found out about this financial lifeline, many withdrew their savings in the first run on a bank in Britain for around 140 years.

Rating the credit agencies

by Elaine Moore

C In response to the Northern Rock crisis in 2007, the UK Parliamentary Treasury committee was fierce. 'You all failed,' was one member's verdict on
5 the role of the credit-rating agencies. Admittedly, with predictions for a global economic slowdown, politicians were keen to find scapegoats. So banks, central banks and regulators all faced
10 criticism for their failure to foresee the consequences of the US subprime mortgage lending crisis.

D One group in particular was heavily criticised. The Treasury Committee
15 interrogated representatives of the three largest credit-rating agencies: Fitch, Moody's and Standard & Poor's (S&P).

E Corporate credit-rating agencies
20 assess the creditworthiness of bonds and bond issuers. They assign different grades to corporate bonds, using their own grading system. The highest-ranked 'investment-grade' bonds are
25 rated triple-A. Those at the lowest end of the spectrum, with 'junk bond' status, are rated either C or D, depending on the agency. Fund managers and other investors use the information
30 to assess the potential return on investment.

F Unfortunately, the agencies had given many assets securitised with subprime mortgages triple-A ratings.
35 When the global credit squeeze hit, their credibility was called into question. Should these assets ever have been given the top rating? Should investors have been warned of the risks
40 earlier? They were accused of reacting too slowly to changing situations and of facing a conflict of interest because they earned a fee from the issuers whose securities they rated.

G In 2007, the US Securities and Exchange Commission (SEC) listed seven credit-rating agencies as nationally recognised statistical rating organisations. Two of these, Japan
50 Credit Rating Agency and Rating and Investment Information, were new additions in June.

H However, the much larger S&P, Moody's and Fitch still dominated the
55 market. This led Jean-Claude Trichet, the President of the European Central Bank, to complain about the lack of choice between global credit-rating agencies. So European Union market
60 watchdogs started questioning the rating agencies about their role in the subprime mortgage crisis, and the International Organisation of Securities Commissions (IOSCO), representing
65 more than 100 securities regulators, set up a taskforce to improve their regulation.

I In their own defence, the rating agencies maintained that their job
70 was to provide an opinion on the probability of a company defaulting on its debt repayments, not market performance. Added to that, they stressed that their ratings should never be used
75 as the sole reason for an investment decision. Furthermore, S&P pointed out that it had reported the 'possible risk' for investors of 'creative financing opportunities within the residential
80 mortgage realm' as early as April 2005. It seemed, however, that nobody had been listening.

FT

VOCABULARY

A Definitions

Match these phrases from the article (1–8) with their meanings (a–h).

1	the Treasury	a)	the government department in charge of the money that a government collects in taxes and from borrowing, and the money that it spends
2	central bank	b)	a company that provides loans of money for people to buy houses
3	corporate credit-rating agency	c)	in Britain, this entity's shares are freely sold and traded with a minimum share capital of £50,000
4	public limited company	d)	a company or bank that makes certain assets or securities such as shares or bonds available for sale
5	mortgage lender	e)	a company that calculates the risk of lending to or investing in a company or its financial products
6	bond issuer	f)	the official bank of a country, which is responsible for setting interest rates, controlling the money supply, producing banknotes and keeping the country's supply of foreign currency and gold
7	subprime mortgage	g)	a restraint or limitation of credit; usually (although not always) a government measure designed to reduce inflation, by methods such as increasing interest rates
8	credit squeeze	h)	a loan to buy a house which has been given to a borrower with a poor credit rating

B Vocabulary development

bond rating		grade	risk	
Moody's	Standard & Poor's			
Aaa	AAA	investment	lowest risk	
Aa	AA	investment	low risk	
A	A	investment	low risk	
Baa	BBB	investment	medium risk	
Ba, B	BB, B	junk	high risk	
Caa/Ca/C	CCC/CC/C	junk	highest risk	
C	D	junk	in default	

Complete the sentences using the chart above and the phrases in the box.

> as risky as   as safe as   considerably safer than   much riskier than
> slightly riskier than   the riskiest / in default   the safest

1 Moody's Caa rating is .... Standard and Poor's CCC rating.
2 An A-rated investment is .... an Aa- or AA-rated investment.
3 An Aaa or AAA rating is ....
4 An Aa or AA rating is .... a Caa or CCC rating.
5 A C or D rating is ....
6 An Aa rating is .... an AA rating.
7 A B rating is .... an AAA rating.

C **Word partnerships**

Match the verbs (1–6) with the noun phrases (a–f) to make expressions similar to those in the article.

1 to assess
2 to assign
3 to default
4 to rate
5 to improve
6 to securitise

a) different grades to corporate bonds
b) corporate bonds and bond issuers
c) the creditworthiness of bonds and issuers
d) on debt repayments
e) an asset
f) regulation

D **Text completion**

1 Use the words in the box to complete the explanation of securitisation below.

| bank   bond   borrower   interest   investor   lender   repayments   securitised |

A financial institution, such as a ....[1] buys a loan from a ....[2] (such as another bank), who has already lent an amount of money to a ....[3] (another person or institution). This means that the financial institution now has the right to collect the ....[4] on the original borrower's loan. It then uses the expectation of receiving these as security for a ....[5], which it issues to an individual or corporate ....[6] in return for a specific amount of money, which the financial institution promises to repay the investor at a later date. The financial institution also uses the original borrower's repayments to make ....[7] payments to the bond holder until the date when the bond is repaid. Both the financial institution who bought the loan and ....[8] it in the form of a bond, and the bank who originally sold the loan to the financial institution, use the capital they have received from their sales to improve their financial situation or increase their activities. They lend that money to more borrowers, and sell on these loans to other institutions, who then securitise them. And so it goes on.

2 Use the words and phrases in the box to complete the paragraph below.

| bond issuers   credit-rating   highest risk   investment-grade securities regulator   subprime mortgages   treasury committee |

The ....[1] which led an inquiry into the Northern Rock financial collapse blamed almost every player in the financial sector. It particularly pointed the finger at the ....-........[2] agencies, who had assigned ....-........[3] credit ratings to bank securities which turned out to be some of the ....[4] investments in the market. These junk-bond grade assets, based on ....[5] (those granted to borrowers who would be unlikely to repay them), were used to fund further loans to customers. It was pointed out that a fundamental problem lay in the fact that credit-rating agencies were paid by the very ....[6] whose corporate bonds they rated. As a result, the International Organisation of Securities Commissions (IOSCO), the global ....[7], was called in to improve regulation of this sector.

OVER TO YOU

Do an online search of the credit ratings of a number of companies or financial institutions which you are interested in. Write a short report, explaining which rating agency has rated each company, which rating each company has received, and why you think this is. Use the chart in Exercise B to help you.

Company insolvency

This unit looks at how a UK company's directors should proceed when their business is experiencing financial difficulties.

Discuss these questions.

1   Do you know of any companies which have gone bankrupt in your region or another region you are interested in? Explain what happened.

2   What do you think happens to a company's assets in this situation? What risks can there be for a company's creditors?

> When a company is unable to pay its debts and goes out of business, we often say that it has *gone bankrupt*. Officially, in a strict legal sense, this term only applies to individuals in the UK, whereas in the US it can apply to both individuals and companies.

A   Understanding the main points

Read the article on the opposite page and answer these questions.

1   What sort of business does the director in this article run?

2   Why is his business experiencing financial difficulties?

3   Which particular problems is he concerned about in relation to his company's current situation?

4   Who is held responsible if a business trades when insolvent?

5   If a company looks like it is going insolvent, who should the directors protect as a first priority?

6   Who should the company directors get advice from if they think they might be going insolvent?

7   What important feature of the company should they also protect?

8   In this situation, what should they also do on a regular basis?

B   Understanding details

Read the article again and answer these questions.

1   What three penalties, or 'remedies', could company directors encounter if they trade while insolvent?

2   Which two documents provide information on how company directors should conduct their business?

3   Which financial documents do company directors use to assess the financial health of their company?

4   Besides the company itself, who should company directors take advice for?

5   If they feel that that the company will be unable to repay future debts, which two things must company directors not do?

6   Who should company directors make sure they don't show preference to when experiencing financial difficulties?

7   What specific actions should company directors take during meetings if their company is experiencing financial difficulties?

A responsible approach to insolvency

by Jonathan Moules

Simon Longfield, restructuring partner at Grant Thornton, an accountancy firm, answers the following question about company insolvency.

A I am a director of a small retail business. My accountant has recently warned me that, following a sharp downturn in trading, the
5 business is unlikely to be able to survive much longer. I am worried about my responsibilities and my financial liabilities if the business becomes insolvent. So what should
10 I be doing right now?

B As soon as the directors of a company foresee, or even become aware of the possibility of, an administration situation, they need to act carefully to
15 avoid the business trading insolvently, as the penalties for doing this can be severe. These 'remedies' may include personal liability for creditors' debts, disqualification as a company
20 director and, in extreme cases, imprisonment where fraudulent trading has taken place.

C So, as a director, how do you protect the company and yourself from such
25 risks if insolvency is possibly imminent? The principal steps include fulfilling the normal duties expected of a company director, which are set out in the constitution (articles) of the
30 company and the Companies Act. Most importantly, the interests of the company's creditors must become a priority.

D Firstly, the directors must understand the company's current financial situa-
35 tion, assess the prospects for its future viability and act quickly on the position they judge the company to be in. They should use the following information to arrive at a judgement of the compa-
40 ny's current position: up-to-date statutory accounts, management accounts and forecasts based on the company's latest order book.

E After that, if the directors decide that
45 their company is moving towards an insolvency position, they need to take independent professional advice from a specialist or licensed insolvency practitioner and, additionally, take
50 advice for themselves personally, if necessary.

F Next, they need to ensure that the assets of the company are always protected and secure and not sold for less
55 than their value. In addition, as well as making sure that they do not take on new supplies or lines of credit that they know the company cannot repay, the directors must be able to show at all
60 times that they are acting in the best interests of all of the company's existing creditors. This last measure is essential to avoid any accusation of special or preferential treatment of
65 specific creditors.

G Finally, directors should hold regular meetings and keep minutes of the discussions they have and the key decisions they make. If there is any
70 doubt about this, they should detail the circumstances that justify continued trading. If they are convinced that the business will be able to 'ride out the storm', then the company and its direc-
75 tors can continue in the normal way.

H However, as soon as they identify that their business is likely to become insolvent, the directors need to act quickly to seek the protection that an
80 insolvency (administration) procedure can offer. It is the job of a licensed insolvency practitioner to help company directors put in place the most suitable procedure – if the business can
85 continue to trade in any way.

VOCABULARY

A Definitions

1 Match these words from the article (1–4) with their meanings (a–d).

1 insolvency   a) when a company which is experiencing financial difficulties is reorganised by an independent specialist with the aim of continuing some of its activities

2 liquidation   b) when a company that is bankrupt is put under the control of an individual by the courts

3 administration   c) when a person or company does not have enough money or assets to pay their debts

4 receivership   d) when a failing company stops operating and its assets are sold to pay its debts

2 Match each word or phrase from the article (1–8) with one which has a similar meaning (a–h).

1 small retail business   a) penalties
2 sharp downturn   b) shop
3 financial liabilities   c) big drop
4 remedies   d) intending to deceive
5 disqualification   e) the amount owed to others
6 fraudulent   f) not allowed to continue doing something
7 minutes   g) the place where agreed future sales are recorded
8 order book   h) notes of what is discussed or agreed during a meeting

B Word partnerships

Match the verbs (1–8) with the phrases (a–h) to make expressions similar to those in the article.

1 to take   a) minutes of major discussions and decisions
2 to become   b) independent professional advice
3 to fulfill   c) directors' duties
4 to assess   d) the company's financial situation
5 to understand   e) the prospects for the company's future viability
6 to trade   f) in the best interests of all of the creditors
7 to keep   g) insolvent
8 to act   h) insolvently

C Sentence completion

Use words and phrases from Exercises A and B to complete these sentences.

1 When economic conditions become difficult, businesses can experience a .... in trading.

2 When a company cannot pay its creditors, it becomes ....

3 The company stopped trading, and its assets were sold to pay off its creditors. It went into ....

4 The directors were hiding financial problems in the company, and after an investigation, their dealings were found to be ....

5   As a result, the directors were subject to severe .... They went to prison.

6   In addition to this, they suffered .... as company directors for several years.

7   It was discovered that some important items in their meetings had not been written down in the ....

8   They had also entered false items into their ...., to make their business look more viable than it actually was.

D   Understanding expressions

Choose the best explanation for each phrase from the article.

1   'As soon as the directors of a company *foresee* ...' (lines 11–12)

   a) predict
   b) experience

2   '... if insolvency is possibly *imminent*?' (lines 25–26)

   a) going to happen very soon
   b) going to happen at some time in the future

3   '... *fulfilling* the normal duties ...' (line 27)

   a) increasing
   b) carrying out

4   '... must *become a priority*.' (line 32)

   a) take first place
   b) be ignored

5   '... the prospects for its future *viability* ...' (lines 35–36)

   a) realistic existence as a business
   b) finding new ways to do business

6   '... will be able to "*ride out the storm*", ...' (lines 73–74)

   a) pay as little as possible
   b) survive the bad period

OVER TO YOU

1   Can you think of any reasons why companies fail? Think of economies, markets, management, competitors, customers and suppliers. Discuss.

2   If a very large company starts to perform badly and looks like it might fail, what sort of 'spin-off' problems can occur? Think of the national or local economy, the directors, the employees, the customers and suppliers and the creditors. Write a short report detailing your ideas.

3   The following sequencing words and phrases are used in the article to order the steps a company director should take in the case of financial difficulty:

   First   After that   Next   Additionally   In addition   Finally

   Use these to give a short presentation on the subject.

This unit looks at the circumstances which led to the rescue of a major UK bank by a rival bank, Lloyds TSB, and the UK taxpayer.

BEFORE YOU READ

Discuss these questions.

1   In terms of risk-taking, how would you expect a bank to act?
2   Do you know of any past banking failures, either in your own country or abroad? If so, describe them briefly.

READING

A   **Understanding the main points**

Read the article on the opposite page and answer these questions.

1   Why were people surprised that Sir James Crosby left HBOS in 2006?
2   What happened to HBOS in 2008?
3   What was Paul Moore's position in the bank before he left in 2005?
4   What did Mr Moore say was wrong with HBOS's growth strategy? Was the bank taking too many risks, or not enough in his opinion?
5   What type of company is HBOS compared to, in terms of its corporate strategy?
6   Who else was worried about the inadequate risk management at HBOS?
7   Which potential economic situation did they fear would expose the weaknesses in HBOS's attitude to risk?

B   **Understanding details**

Read the article again and answer these questions.

1   Which position did Sir James Crosby hold at HBOS until 2006?
2   Which position did Sir James eventually take up after he left HBOS?
3   Which two banks merged in 2001 to form HBOS?
4   How did the main funding policy of the two banks differ, before they merged?
5   What had happened when Mr Moore had tried to highlight the dangers of the bank's growth strategies in the past?
6   Which two business sectors did analysts feel that HBOS had lent too much money to?
7   What was their specific concern about the UK property market?

Evidence triggered Crosby's departure

by Jane Croft

A When Sir James Crosby, CEO, left Halifax Bank of Scotland (HBOS), one of the world's largest banks, in 2006, many were surprised that he had chosen to leave a top job in British banking so young. The bank's shares had hit an all-time peak, and its financial results appeared to be excellent.

B Today, however, his exit from the bank at only 50 years old looks more like a fortunate piece of timing. After the 'credit crunch', which later developed into a full-blown recession, hit in 2008, HBOS was on the point of collapse.

C Paul Moore, Head of Regulatory Risk at HBOS between 2002 and 2005, made a statement to UK Members of Parliament in mid-February 2009. This started the chain of events that ended in Sir James's resignation as Deputy Chairman of the Financial Services Authority (FSA), an appointment made by the UK government treasury under Gordon Brown. He said that under Sir James's leadership, HBOS was 'going too fast' and was a 'serious risk to financial stability'.

D The origins of the bank's aggressive approach to doing business can be found in the merger of Halifax and Bank of Scotland in 2001. The logic of putting the two businesses together was this: Bank of Scotland, which relied on wholesale (borrowed) funding to finance at least half its lending, could utilise Halifax's larger balance sheet and retail deposits (made by savers) to increase corporate lending.

E HBOS adopted Bank of Scotland's aggressive funding model. Halifax, as a former building society, had been around 80-per-cent funded by retail deposits. But as the new entity grew, it relied more on wholesale funding than retail deposits to finance growth. It grew very speedily on the back of the consumer lending boom in the early 2000s.

F Sir James also hired Mr Hornby, a former supermarket executive, to develop the retail bank, and HBOS became an aggressive competitor, offering supermarket-style 'pile them high, sell them cheap' products, in line with their sales-driven business culture.

G Mr Moore said in evidence, 'I told the board they should slow down, but was prevented from having this properly minuted by the Chief Financial Officer. I told them their sales culture was significantly out of balance with their systems and controls,' allegations which HBOS denied.

H As far back as 2003, however, some analysts had expressed concerns that HBOS was expanding too quickly and taking on too much risk, particularly in financing various retail and real-estate entrepreneurs. It added to the group's bet on UK property through private equity-style deals to buy into builders, hotels and restaurants as the market neared its peak.

I One analyst wrote in 2003, 'HBOS has grown its [corporate] loan book significantly faster than other large banks. As long as the economy is robust, HBOS has great revenue potential, but there are risks if we face a slowdown.' In 2002 alone, HBOS lent £5.5bn to commercial property – more than the entire loan exposure to commercial property of rival Lloyds TSB.

J Although the crisis in wholesale markets hit all banks, HBOS's wholesale funding policy and exposure to the UK property market left it more vulnerable than other banks. Mr Moore's claims provide some ideas as to why the bank came so close to collapse in 2008.

FT

C **Understanding meaning**

1 In paragraph 1, the author mentions that Sir James Crosby's departure from the head of the bank at such a young age (50) now looks like a 'fortunate piece of timing'. What might she be implying by this phrase?

2 In paragraph G, when Paul Moore told the bank that their sales culture was 'significantly out of balance with their systems and controls', which banking function was he referring to?

3 The article mentions that HBOS lent a lot of money to the property market: *It added to the bet on UK property* (paragraph H). What type of activity does the word bet normally relate to? What does this suggest about the bank's approach to business?

4 As long ago as 2003, a number of people expressed concerns about HBOS's business strategy. Find an expression in paragraph I of the article which describes how HBOS was 'expanding too quickly' compared to other banks.

VOCABULARY

A Definitions

Match these phrases from the article (1–6) with their meanings (a–f).

1	wholesale funding	a)	money which is lent to private individuals
2	retail deposits	b)	a (debt) method that banks use in addition to savers' deposits to finance operations
3	consumer lending	c)	a financial institution which was originally formed to help people buy or build houses with money which was saved with it
4	corporate lending	d)	the money that savers put into banks
5	building society	e)	the total amount of money a financial institution has lent to customers
6	loan exposure	f)	money which is lent to companies

B Vocabulary development

Without looking back at the article, tick (✓) the statements which are found in it.

1 The bank's shares had hit an all-time peak. ☐
2 The bank's shares had hit an all-time low. ☐
3 Its financial results were disappointing. ☐
4 Its financial results appeared to be excellent. ☐
5 HBOS shares bottomed out. ☐
6 HBOS was on the point of collapse. ☐
7 HBOS's share price doubled in a week. ☐
8 It grew very speedily. ☐
9 HBOS was contracting too quickly. ☐
10 HBOS was expanding too quickly. ☐

C Definitions

Match these words and phrases from the article (1–8) with their meanings (a–h).

1	all-time peak	a)	a time when business activity increases rapidly
2	credit crunch	b)	strong and stable
3	recession	c)	a reduction in the general availability of loans or credit or a sudden tightening of the conditions required to obtain a loan from the banks
4	collapse	d)	a period when demand for products and services decreases
5	boom	e)	at risk, open to danger
6	robust (economy)	f)	the reduction of a country's gross domestic product (GDP), usually for at least two quarters of a year
7	economic slowdown	g)	when something such as a share reaches its highest historical point, price or value
8	vulnerable	h)	when a company, organisation or system suddenly fails or becomes too weak to continue

D Sentence completion

Use words and phrases from Exercises A–C to complete these sentences.

1 In 2008, the UK experienced a........ ...., which meant that people found it more difficult to get a loan from a bank.

2 In 2006, HBOS shares had........ an all-time......... By 2008, however, the picture was quite different. The bank was on the........ of.........

3 HBOS had adopted a very aggressive funding model which left it very........ when the credit crunch hit.

4 The bank had relied too heavily on........ .... and not enough on........ deposits.

5 Added to that, the bank's sales-driven culture had resulted in the bank having an extremely high........ .... It had lent far too much money to customers.

6 The economic........ was over and what was first believed to be a short credit crunch had turned into a more serious.........

E Understanding expressions

Choose the best explanation for each phrase from the article.

1 '... Sir James's *resignation as* Deputy Chairman ...' (lines 21–22)
   a) when someone leaves their job voluntarily
   b) when someone is fired by their employer

2 '... *on the back of the* consumer lending boom ...' (lines 48–49)
   a) as a result of
   b) after

3 '... "*pile them high, sell them cheap*" products ...' (lines 55–56)
   a) a few products with a high profit margin
   b) a lot of products with a low profit margin

4 ' ... from having this properly *minuted* ...' (lines 61–62)
   a) time spent on it
   b) written down in the official notes of the meeting

OVER TO YOU

1 In banking, what are the pros and cons of having a very strict risk-management policy? Think of different economic conditions, different forms of funding, different types of lending and the part these can play in the success (or failure!) of a bank. Give a short presentation.

2 The disgrace of troubled UK banks extends further than this story. Several executives of troubled banks were heavily criticised for trying to accept enormous financial payments, even after these institutions had got into serious financial difficulty. Should an executive of a failed bank be allowed to carry on taking so much money? How should such executives be dealt with? Discuss your ideas.

3 Do an online search to discover what has become of HBOS and its other senior executives since this article was written. Give a short presentation.

4 Did a bank in your region suffer difficulties? If so, describe the events in a brief report.

This unit looks at the different opinions UK auditors can give on a company's financial report.

Discuss these questions.

1 In general, how important do you think the audit report is to a company's investors? Do they understand or even bother to read it?

2 How do you think the shareholders of a company which received a negative opinion about its annual financial statements would react? Would this opinion have any effect on the company's future?

> Many large UK companies' annual financial statements are audited by a firm of external auditors. The auditor's opinions are published in the audit report, included in a company's annual report.

READING

A **Understanding the main points**

Read the article on the opposite page and say whether these statements are true (T) or false (F). Identify the part of the article that gives this information.

1 In general, investors pay careful attention to the auditors' report on a company.

2 A negative auditors' opinion indicates that the auditors disagree with the statements that a company's directors have made about it.

3 In difficult economic times, investors might react more strongly to a negative opinion, to the extent that they push the company into complete failure.

4 Auditors are not held responsible if they fail to indicate that a company's financial affairs look unhealthy, then the company goes bankrupt.

5 Financial regulators require auditors to clearly indicate a company's poor financial outlook.

6 Poor economic conditions make auditors even more cautious when writing their report.

B **Understanding details**

Read the article again and answer these questions.

1 When do the majority of UK companies have their year end?

2 How long is an auditor's opinion on a company valid for?

3 What is the worst opinion an auditor can give?

4 What does every company want its auditor to give it?

5 Which paragraph alerts investors to important information?

6 Which two phrases might auditors put before this paragraph?

7 Which series of events in 2001 was very costly for audit firms?

Scary jargon in a jittery market

by Jennifer Hughes

A Auditors' jargon rarely enters normal conversation but one phrase – 'added emphasis' – has the power to terrify boardrooms. It is a phrase that audit-
5 ors sometimes use to indicate possible dangers hiding below the surface of a company's balance sheet.

B Every January, just after the books close for more than half the UK's top
10 companies, investors begin the wait for the full-year financial statements. Most years, the auditor's report – a page of largely standardised phrases, including an opinion of whether the business
15 is a valid going concern – attracts little interest. In a bad year, however, that 'going concern' statement is criti-cal to investors.

C Technically, 'going-concern appro-
20 val' means that the auditors consider the business to be viable for at least a year from when the accounts are signed off. At worst, auditors can give an 'adverse opinion', indicating a general

25 and serious disagreement with the directors' statement of the company's financial position. In volatile markets, however, even a 'qualified opinion', indicating a limited and specific
30 concern, can act as a death warning.

D Rather than a 'qualified opinion', an auditor's report is more likely to include 'emphasis of matter' para-graphs, which are designed to draw
35 investors' attention to crucial disclo-sures. In difficult times, you see more of these in audit reports.

E Says Steve Maslin, a partner at Grant Thornton, a large firm of accountants,
40 'Take the case where you don't dis-agree that the business is a going concern, but there is an important dis-closure, perhaps about the company's financing facilities for the next year.
45 You want to tell investors "you need to read and understand Note 27". So we'll add a paragraph in the report [to high-light this fact].'

F In auditing standards, these 'empha-
50 ses' are preceded by terrifying phrases

such as 'significant level of concern' and 'material uncertainty'. 'The word-ing is horrid. There is a danger that the market will react to this and it will
55 become a self-fulfilling prophecy,' says Martyn Jones, National Audit Techni-cal Partner at Deloitte.

G Auditors have good reason to worry about professional liability. After the
60 failure of many dotcom companies in 2001, a wave of lawsuits against audit firms followed. Since then, regulators have made it clear they will take a firm line with audit firms. 'There are no
65 excuses these days for saying "when we signed off, we didn't think about that,"' said Paul Boyle, Chief Execu-tive of the Financial Reporting Council in a warning issued to the FTSE 350.

H In a difficult economic environment, investors can start to panic at any delay in the publishing of the annual report, so the nightmare scenario is a last-minute hitch in the financing plans
75 – without which the auditors will not sign off a clean opinion. Take the situ-ation 'where a client is heavily dependent on a bank facility and the bank suddenly wants last-minute infor-
80 mation. You end up having meetings late into the night,' says Mr Ratcliffe, an audit partner at PwC.

I This means that, despite auditors' best efforts to prepare, the outcome is
85 not in their hands. So in a difficult year, auditors are even more rigorous than usual. No matter how well-run the cli-ent company is, a year of difficult economic conditions is the year you sit
90 down and make sure you really, really understand that bank mandate or those liabilities.

FT

VOCABULARY

A Word search

Find words or phrases in the article which fit these definitions.

1 the technical vocabulary that a certain industry or profession uses (title)
   j........

2 volatile, nervous (title)
   j........

3 what the phrases in an audit report are said to be when the wording of opinions varies very little from one report to another (paragraph B)
   s........

4 what the accounts are said to be when a company's financial accounts have been inspected and the auditors have found them to give a true and fair view of the company's finances (paragraph C)
   s........ o........

5 extra information which the directors of a company give in the notes to the financial report (paragraph D)
   d........

6 a company which does business using the Internet or provides an Internet service (paragraph G)
   d........

7 a charge, complaint or claim against a company or person made in a court of law.
   Several audit firms suffered these after the dotcom crash in 2001. (paragraph G)
   l........

8 when auditors are satisfied that a company is in good financial health for the coming year (paragraph H)
   c........ o........

9 an arrangement made by a bank for its customers which lets them borrow money (paragraph H)
   b........ f........

10 an official instruction given to a person or organisation by a bank, allowing them to do something (paragraph I)
   b........ m........

B Definitions

Match these phrases from the article (1–4) with their meanings (a–d).

1 going concern

2 emphasis of matter

3 qualified opinion

4 adverse opinion

a) given in an audit if the auditor disagrees with the treatment or disclosure of a specific piece of information in the financial statements, or if the auditor feels that the audit has been too limited in its scope

b) a business that functions without the intention or threat of liquidation for the next 12 months

c) when the auditor decides that the financial statements of a company are materially misstated and, when considered as a whole, do not conform with the generally accepted accounting principles in force at the time (such as IFRS)

d) a paragraph which draws attention to a specific point disclosed in a company's financial statement which the auditor considers to be of great importance to the user's understanding of the statement

C Sentence completion

Use words and phrases from Exercises A and B to complete these sentences.

1 The auditors were very pleased to give the company their ....-........ approval for the next year.

2 Therefore, they .... its financial report.

3 The banks were having financial difficulties and called the company's directors to a meeting to discuss its .... for the coming year.

4 The auditors were satisfied in general with PRQ company's accounts, but in their report, they drew attention to a specific .... in an .... of .... paragraph.

5 The auditors were totally dissatisfied with the financial affairs of XYZ company. They gave an .... in their report.

D Understanding expressions

Choose the best explanation for each phrase from the article.

1 '... it will *become a self-fulfilling prophecy* ...' (lines 54–55)
   a) actually make the disaster happen
   b) describe the disaster

2 '... *a wave* of lawsuits ...' (line 61)
   a) a small number   b) a large number

3 '... they will *take a firm line with* audit firms.' (lines 63–64)
   a) create a new audit firm   b) be very strict with

4 '... the nightmare scenario is a *last-minute hitch* ...' (lines 73–74)
   a) a problem which occurs late in the process
   b) a last-minute drop in the company's share price

5 '... *the outcome is not in their hands*.' (lines 84–85)
   a) they are not responsible for the final result
   b) they are not responsible for what they publish

6 '... even more *rigorous* than usual.' (lines 86–87)
   a) difficult   b) careful and thorough

OVER TO YOU

1 Do an Internet search for examples of companies which have received a qualified opinion or an emphasis-of-matter paragraph in their audit report. Write a short summary of the reasons for this.

2 This article was based on the situation which auditors and companies were facing at the end of 2008, as the 'credit crunch' had actually turned into a full economic recession. The audit firms were clearly anxious about how they should report on companies' financial statements in the light of the likely liquidity problems being faced by some companies. Visit the UK Financial Reporting Council's website at www.frc.org.uk and read the Auditing Practices Board's (APB) December 2008 bulletin (2008/10), entitled 'Going Concern Issues During the Current Economic Conditions'. Write a short summary of the APB's guidance on how auditors should approach the writing of their audit reports in the near future.

This unit looks at the UK audit firms' battle to reduce their legal and financial responsibility for clients who fail due to fraud or negligence.

Discuss these questions.

1 Why are auditors supposed to remain independent of the directors of the company they are auditing?

2 Who pays an audit firm for its services? Do you think this could create any potential conflicts of interest?

A **Understanding the main points**

Read the article on the opposite page and say whether these statements are true (T) or false (F). Identify the part of the article that gives this information.

1 The UK audit firms were trying to limit their financial risk.

2 The process was an easy one.

3 The outcome of their mission would be decided not only by the British regulators and investors, but also by French ones.

4 By the end of the period described in the article, the auditors had achieved their goal.

B **How the text is organised**

Read the article again and put these events in the correct sequence.

a) The UK government issued a public consultation document on limiting auditors' liability.

b) The proposals to set a limit on a firms' liability only after agreement by a company's shareholders were not opposed by the investment community.

c) The next UK Companies Act allowed audit firms to limit their liability to their proportion of blame by shareholder resolution, once a year.

d) Auditors had total financial responsibility if their clients went bankrupt due to fraud or negligence.

e) The ICAEW got a legal opinion, and the FRC published a set of guidelines to help company directors write legally satisfactory proposals to limit auditor liability, which they could put to their shareholders at the annual general meeting.

f) The SEC raised objections to the changes.

g) Audit firms were permitted to become limited liability partnerships.

h) Company directors became anxious about liability limitation and started a big legal debate about whether they could carry out the permitted changes.

i) The institutional investor community didn't agree with the government's consultation document and rejected it.

Professional liability: Solution faces threat

by **Robert Bruce**

A The arguments about auditor liability had run for decades. But every time a possible solution to the auditors' problem had been found, it had eventually been rejected. Now, the latest attempt to allow UK audit firms to agree specific limits on their liability was in the hands of a US regulator.

B The Securities & Exchange Commission – which has jurisdiction over UK companies that are listed in the US or have raised money in US markets – objected that the proposed deal might not be in investors' interests.

C In the past, if a company failed as the result of negligence or fraud, the auditors had sole financial responsibility. It seemed that no one else would be sued, no matter how guilty. The auditors were seen as having very deep pockets.

D 'It was dishonest,' says Peter Wyman, Global Leader for Public Policy and Regulation at PwC, 'and it was not sustainable. Auditors do not have unlimited funds.' Jan Babiak, Regulatory and Public Policy Managing Partner with Ernst & Young UK, agrees.

E Legal reform proceeded slowly and with many setbacks. The first step was to allow firms to become limited liability partnerships, in line with the US model. That took years to achieve. The next step was to allow them to cap their liability. The government issued a consultation document. However, the institutional investor community persuaded it that this was not in consumers' interests, and the proposal was rejected.

F Only one option remained. This was to limit firms' liability to their proportion of blame in any future case of negligence, on a contractual basis, company by company. The investment community was happy with it, so the government supported it, and proposals were incorporated into the next UK Companies Act.

G Nobody objected until after the Act was passed. Implementation would not be automatic across all companies. Each board of directors would have to put an auditors' liability limitation proposal to a vote at their next annual general meeting. Directors started to worry about shareholder opposition. They would be unable to benefit from the auditors' deep pockets in the event of corporate failure. 'There was a big legal debate over whether directors would be acting in the interests of shareholders if they proposed a limitation resolution,' says Richard Bennison, Head of UK Audit at KPMG.

H As a result, the profession's main body, the Institute of Chartered Accountants of England & Wales (ICAEW), stepped in to obtain a legal opinion. Then, to help persuade directors that this was the right course of action, the Financial Reporting Council (FRC) published guidance to directors along with recommended wording to be used in the proposed resolutions to their investors. This seemed to have solved the problem.

I It was at this point that the SEC arrived on the scene. The main US regulatory authority, aware of its jurisdiction over certain UK companies, became anxious. It saw the possibility of conspiracies between auditors and directors and objected that this would not be in investors' interests.

J 'The SEC fears a "cosy deal" between directors and auditors,' said Mr Wyman. 'But in UK legislation, it is an agreement between auditors and shareholders. It is not a "cosy deal" at all. It is totally transparent.' Everything was on hold once again.

FT

C **Understanding details**

Read the article again and answer these questions.

1 In which two situations does the SEC have the right to object to certain legal matters affecting UK companies?

2 Why weren't the UK auditors happy about the degree of liability they held in the case of failure of a company due to fraud or negligence?

3 Which country provided the model for limited liability partnerships in the UK?

4 Under the new UK Companies Act, would all audit firms automatically benefit from liability limitation?

5 Whose interests did the company directors say they were trying to protect when they started to debate the changes to the Companies Act?

6 Which two UK financial organisations tried to provide a solution to these company directors' problems?

7 What was the SEC concerned about when it opposed the act?

VOCABULARY

A Word families

Complete the chart.

verb	noun
........¹	solution
reject	........²
achieve	........³
object	........⁴
........⁵	limitation
........⁶	implementation
........⁷	proposal
........⁸	opposition

B Word partnerships

Match the verbs (1–8) with the phrases (a–h) to make expressions similar to those in the article.

1 to achieve   a) financial responsibility

2 to have jurisdiction   b) proportional limitation of liability

3 to have sole   c) a consultation document

4 to cap   d) over companies listed in the US

5 to issue   e) a resolution

6 to propose   f) liability

7 to put a proposal   g) a legal opinion

8 to obtain   h) to the vote

C Understanding expressions

Choose the best explanation for each word or phrase from the article.

1 '... which has *jurisdiction* over ...' (line 10)

   a) responsibility for a company's financial management

   b) the official right and power to make decisions about something

2 '... as the result of *negligence* ...' (lines 15–16)

   a) theft

   b) failure to take enough care over something that you are responsible for, for which you may have to pay damages

3 '... or *fraud* ...' (line 16)

   a) a method of illegally getting money from a person or organisation

   b) stealing money from a company

4 '... no one else would be *sued* ...' (lines 18–19)

   a) fired

   b) taken to court

5 '... to become *limited liability partnerships* ...' (lines 32–33)

   a) partnerships in which individual partners are not held legally and financially responsible for their defective audit opinions

   b) partnerships in which individual partners are protected from the risk of personal bankruptcy if they are not personally responsible for a defective audit opinion

6 '... *on a contractual basis* ...' (line 45)

   a) by temporary (renewable) agreement

   b) by permanent agreement

7 'There was a big *legal debate* over ...' (lines 61–62)

   a) illegal action

   b) argument or discussion about a point of law

D Text completion

Use words and phrases from Exercises A–C to complete this paragraph.

The UK audit firms were trying to achieve proportional l........[1] of their l........[2]. They thought that it was very unfair that they should have s........ f........ r........[3] in the event of the failure of a company they had audited in the previous 12 months. The Companies Act allowed auditors to propose a liability limitation r........[4] to shareholders at a company's annual general meeting. The resolution would not be permanent. It would only be agreed by a company's shareholders on a c........ b........[5] once a year. This solution had been arrived at after much l........ d........[6] and a l........ o........[7], provided by experts. However, the process was stopped in its tracks once again. The US Stock Exchange Commission, which had j........[8] over many large UK companies, objected to the idea.

E Word search

Find phrases in the article which fit these meanings.

1 was up to (somebody) to decide (paragraph A)

2 were considered to have unlimited funds (paragraph C)

3 it couldn't be continued (paragraph D)

4 with many breaks in progress (paragraph E)

5 to place a maximum limit on their liability (paragraph E)

6 a euphemism for *conspiracy* (paragraph J)

OVER TO YOU

1 Do you think that audit firms should be totally liable for a client company which fails due to fraud or negligence, or is auditors' limited liability fair? Are there any potential risks in allowing the same accountancy firm to provide lucrative consultancy services to a company which it also audits? Explain your opinions in a short talk.

2 Do an online search to find out if there have been any developments in this story since this article was written. Write a short report.

This unit looks at a typical UK company audit report. It is a report on Vodafone Group plc, a UK company, prepared by Deloitte & Touche LLP.

BEFORE YOU READ

Discuss this question.

In contrast with many English written texts, a typical audit report contains very few reference words such as *it* and *them*. Instead, full names are repeated throughout the report. Why do you think this is?

READING

A **Understanding the main points**

Read the audit report on the opposite page and say whether these statements are true (T) or false (F). Identify the part of the report that gives this information.

1 The profit-and-loss (income) statement for the year ended 31 March 2009 of the parent Company of Vodafone Plc has been audited. (paragraph A)
2 The auditors have used their own set of rules. (paragraph D)
3 The auditors give their opinion as to whether the parent Company Financial Statements give a 'true and fair' view. (paragraph E)
4 They also report as to whether the parent Company Financial Statements have been properly prepared in accordance with the Companies Act 1975. (paragraph E)
5 In addition, the audit report states whether the auditors believe that the Directors' Report reflects the true state of the company's situation. (paragraph E)
6 The auditors only need to consider and report on information published in the annual report. (paragraph G)

B **Understanding details**

Read the report again and answer these questions.

1 Which two financial statements have been reported on separately? (paragraphs A and B)
2 In which part of the annual report are the specific accounting policies, followed by the company in preparing this report, explained? (paragraph A)
3 In which three ways could a company's financial statements seriously misrepresent its true financial situation? (paragraph E)
4 Which three specific issues does the audit firm state it would report on if it were not satisfied with them, according to this report? (paragraph F)
5 Which organisation issued the International Standards on Auditing? (paragraph H)
6 In the auditors' opinion, do these financial statements give a true and fair view of the company's finances? (paragraph J)
7 Do they comply with the Companies Act 1985? (paragraph J)
8 Are the auditors happy with the information contained in the Directors' Report? (paragraph J)

Audit Report on the Company Financial Statements

1 ....

A We have audited the parent Company Financial Statements of Vodafone Group Plc for the year ended 31 March 2008, which comprise the balance sheet and the related notes 1 to 10. These parent Company Financial Statements have been
5 prepared under the accounting policies set out therein.

B We have reported separately on the Consolidated Financial Statements of Vodafone Group Plc for the year ended 31 March 2008 and on the information in the directors' remuneration report that is described as having been
10 audited.

2 ....

C The directors' responsibilities for preparing the Annual Report and the parent Company Financial Statements in accordance with applicable law and United Kingdom Accounting Standards (United Kingdom Generally
15 Accepted Accounting Practice) are set out in the Statement of Directors' Responsibilities.

D Our responsibility is to audit the parent Company Financial Statements in accordance with relevant legal and regulatory requirements and International Standards on Auditing
20 (UK and Ireland).

E We report to you our opinion as to whether the parent Company Financial Statements give a true and fair view and whether the parent Company Financial Statements have been properly prepared in accordance with the Companies
25 Act 1985. We also report to you whether in our opinion the Directors' Report is consistent with the parent Company Financial Statements.

F In addition, we report to you if, in our opinion, the Company has not kept proper accounting records, if we
30 have not received all the information and explanations we require for our audit, or if information specified by law regarding directors' remuneration and other transactions is not disclosed.

G We read the information contained in the Annual Report
35 for the above year as described in the contents section and consider whether it is consistent with the audited parent Company Financial Statements. We consider the implications for our report if we become aware of any apparent misstatements or material inconsistencies with the parent
40 Company Financial Statements. Our responsibility does not extend to any further information outside the annual report.

3 ....

H We conducted our audit in accordance with International Standards on Auditing (UK and Ireland) issued by the Auditing Practices Board. An audit includes examination, on a test
45 basis, of evidence relevant to the amounts and disclosures in the parent Company Financial Statements. It also includes an assessment of the significant estimates and judgements made by the directors in the preparation of the parent Company Financial Statements, and of whether the accounting policies
50 are appropriate to the Company's circumstances, consistently applied and adequately disclosed.

I We planned and performed our audit so as to obtain all the information and explanations which we considered necessary in order to provide us with sufficient evidence to
55 give reasonable assurance that the parent Company Financial Statements are free from material misstatement, whether caused by fraud or other irregularity or error. In forming our opinion, we also evaluated the overall adequacy of the presentation of information in the parent Company
60 Financial Statements.

4 ....

J In our opinion:
- the parent Company Financial Statements give a true and fair view, in accordance with United Kingdom Generally Accepted Accounting Practice, of the
65 state of the Company's affairs as at 31 March 2008;
- the parent Company Financial Statements have been properly prepared in accordance with the Companies Act 1985; and
- the information given in the Directors' Report is consistent
70 with the parent Company Financial Statements.

C **How the text is organised**

Read the report again and decide which section (1–4) each of these headings should go with.

a) Opinion
b) Respective responsibilities of directors and auditors
c) Independent auditor's report to the members of Vodafone Group plc
d) Basis of audit opinion

VOCABULARY

A   Word search

Find words or phrases in the report which fit these meanings.

1   phrase which describes exactly which year's accounts have been audited (paragraph A)

f........ t........ y........ e........

2   adjective which describes the financial statements which have been prepared for the entire group of companies, rather than just the parent company (paragraph B)

c........

3   document in which the directors explain how they pay themselves (paragraph B)

d........ r........ r........

4   statement which explains the duties that the directors of a company have to prepare legal and accurate financial statements (paragraph C)

S........ of D........ R........

5   when the law requires or states something (paragraph F)

s........ by l........

6   false statements by the directors in the audit report (paragraph G)

m........

7   significant differences between what the auditors believe to be the company's true financial state and the information given by the directors in the annual report (paragraph G)

m........ i........

8   what the auditors have to do to get the general picture because they cannot examine every single transaction or calculation behind the figures in a company's financial statements (paragraph H)

check on a t........ b........

9   description of the auditors' view on the accuracy of important forecasts made and decisions taken by the directors on the company's behalf (paragraph H)

significant e........ and j........

10   what the auditors provide because they can't state with absolute certainty that the company's accounts are totally accurate and fair (paragraph (I))

r........ a........

B   Definitions

Match these phrases from paragraph H of the report (1–3) with their meanings (a–c).

1   ... policies are *appropriate to the Company's circumstances* ...

2   ... the Company's circumstances, *consistently applied* and ...

3   ... and *adequately disclosed*.

a)   The company *hasn't switched* from one accounting policy to another.

b)   The company has followed policies which *fit its trading and financial situation*.

c)   The company's accounting policies have been *explained clearly enough* for investors.

C Synonyms

Match each word or phrase from the article (1–6) with one which has a similar meaning (a–f).

1 comprise (line 3)
2 set out therein (line 5)
3 in accordance with (line 13)
4 applicable (line 13)
5 consistent with (line 26)
6 so as to (line 52)

a) in force or in effect
b) consist of
c) in agreement with
d) written out in them
e) conforming to
f) in order to

D Text completion

Use words and phrases from Exercises A–C to complete this extract from an audit report for ABC Group Plc.

We have audited the parent Company Financial Statements of ABC Group Plc .... the ....[1] 31 March 20XX which ....[2] the balance sheet and the related notes 1 to 15. These parent Company Financial Statements have been prepared under the accounting policies ....[3] therein.

We report to you our opinion as to whether the parent Company Financial Statements give a true and fair view and whether the parent Company Financial Statements have been properly prepared ....[4] the Companies Act 1985. We also report to you whether in our opinion the Directors' Report is ....[5] the parent Company Financial Statements.

We conducted our audit in accordance with International Standards on Auditing (UK and Ireland) issued by the Auditing Practices Board. An audit includes examination, on a ....[6], of evidence relevant to the amounts and disclosures in the parent Company Financial Statements. It also includes an assessment of the significant .... and ....[7] made by the directors in the preparation of the parent Company Financial Statements, and of whether the accounting policies are ....[8] to the Company's circumstances, consistently applied and adequately disclosed.

We planned and performed our audit ....[9] obtain all the information and explanations which we considered necessary in order to provide us with sufficient evidence to give ....[10] that the parent Company Financial Statements are free from material ....[11] or ....[12] whether caused by fraud or other irregularity or error.

OVER TO YOU

1 What sort of qualities do you think a good auditor should have? Do you think auditing could be an interesting career for a qualified accountant? Could there be any spin-off career opportunities for experienced auditors? Explain your ideas in a short report.
2 Go to www.youtube.com to find videocasts about accounting and auditing careers.

A **Use words and phrases from Units 1–9 to complete these sentences.**

1 A company which is no longer able to pay its debts needs to consult an i........ practitioner.

2 A f........ accountant investigates whether illegal financial activity has taken place in a company.

3 The set of accounting standards which is being adopted in many countries is called the I........ F........ R........ S.........

4 A company's k........ a........ p........ guide its accounting procedures and practices.

5 A l........ is money borrowed from a bank on which interest is usually payable.

6 R........ are a company's profits from previous periods which have not been paid to shareholders.

7 D........ is the amount by which the value of a fixed asset goes down each year.

8 D........ is a part of the profits of a company for a particular period of time that is paid to shareholders of each share that they own.

9 G........ is the value that a company has in addition to its assets, such as its reputation.

10 When business activity increases during an economic downturn, it is called 'c........-c........'.

11 Companies whose business takes time to react to changing economic conditions, are known as l........-c........ companies.

12 The I........ A........ S........ B........ is an organisation which has the aim of making accounting rules the same all over the world.

13 A competitor made a h........ bid for a company which did not want to be taken over.

14 Corporate f........ like to take advantage of interesting business investment opportunities.

15 A person who starts a new company is called an e.........

16 To set up a new company you need money, known as 'c........'.

17 Investors are happiest when they receive a high r........ of r........ on their investments.

18 Arranging finances in a clever, profitable and sometimes slightly dishonest way is known as f........ e.........

19 Companies which borrow money usually have to provide the lender with some type of security or c........ in case they cannot repay the loan.

20 If a company makes a lot of cash, this can be called generating l.........

B **Choose the best word or phrase to complete each of these sentences.**

1 CIMA, ACCA and ICAEW are all accounting.........
   a) professions   b) institutes   c) rules   d) policies

2 The Financial Services Authority is the financial........ of all providers of financial services in the UK.
   a) institute   b) training centre   c) regulator   d) court

3 An........ is something owned by a company which has the power to make money.
   a) asset   b) auditor   c) account   d) exposure

4 A........ is an amount of money owed by a company to a lender of supplier.
   a) dividend   b) debtor   c) deposit   d) liability

5 .... is the capital that a company has from shares rather than from loans.
   a) Securities   b) Equity   c) Retained profit   d) Earnings per share

6 A company's .... profit is the profit relating to its normal activities of providing goods or services.

   a) paper b) pre-tax c) trading d) operating

7 Companies regularly publish performance forecasts or ....

   a) expectations b) guidance c) predictions d) considerations

8 A strong or .... currency or stock performs well when others are doing badly.

   a) reliable b) powerful c) resilient d) solid

9 In response to the banking crisis, banks were allowed to change from the fair-value method to the .... cost method for valuing certain assets.

   a) amortised b) advanced c) adapted d) actual

10 Another name for an industry regulator is a ....

   a) director b) supervisor c) council d) watchdog

11 When the value of stocks and shares is rising and falling without much warning, this is known as market ....

   a) instability b) volatility c) risk d) shakiness

12 When a company reduces the value of an asset on its balance sheet, it writes it ....

   a) off b) on c) down d) up

13 Good .... management helps to protect a company from financial disaster.

   a) cost b) quality c) people d) risk

14 China has engaged in more .... in recent years.

   a) financial speculation b) lending c) foreign investment d) borrowing

15 A new company is called a start-......... .

   a) off b) out c) in d) up

16 Potential investors in a new company want to see a strong business ....

   a) project b) history c) account d) plan

17 When some of a company's managers take over part of the company and run it separately, this is known as a ....

   a) merger b) management buyout c) hostile takeover d) golden parachute

18 Options and futures are types of ....

   a) debts b) accounts c) derivatives d) strategies

19 The amount of money a lender has lent, which it could risk losing, is known as ....

   a) exposure b) credit c) collateral d) debt

20 If a company borrows money to fund the major part of an investment, the investment is said to be highly ....

   a) risky b) leveraged c) subsidised d) costly

A **Use words and phrases from Units 10–18 to complete these sentences.**

1 Even large companies are becoming concerned about s......... They want to reduce the negative impact of their activities on the environment.

2 Environmental issues can now be f........ e........ in the normal reporting processes of a company.

3 Something which changes the decision-making process in a company is said to have a s........ impact on it.

4 Sustainability is now used in many companies as a business p........ driver.

5 Investing simply in order to make a quick profit on a rising stock is described as engaging in price s..........

6 Environmentally conscious companies use a sustainable s........ chain.

7 Large companies which invest large amounts of money in shares are i........ investors.

8 Companies have to make certain items of information public by law. This is known as a corporate d........ requirement.

9 When the value of a person's shares no longer provides enough equity to cover a percentage of the money they have borrowed from the share broker to buy them, the broker will put out a m........ call, requiring additional funds from the borrower, forcing the automatic sale of some shares.

10 The official bank of a country, which is responsible for producing banknotes, making money available and keeping the country's supply of gold, is known as its c........ bank.

11 A mortgage granted to a borrower whose credit history is not sufficient to obtain a conventional mortgage is known as a s........ mortgage.

12 When a company that is bankrupt is put under the control of an individual by the courts, it is said to be in r..........

13 In an economic downturn, the number of cases of f........ activity on the part of companies is expected to rise, as they try to deceive investors and creditors.

14 The amounts of money which savers put in banks are known as retail d..........

15 A period of time when an economy is doing badly and business decreases is known as a r..........

16 A charge, claim or complaint against a person or company which is made in a court of law by a person or company is a l..........

17 An official instruction given to a person or organisation by a bank, allowing them to do something is called a b........ m..........

18 The official right and power to make decisions over something is known as j..........

19 If, according to the auditors, a company's directors say things which are not true in the financial accounts, the auditors refer to it as a m..........

20 Significant differences between a company's true position and the picture that the directors give are known as m........ i..........

B **Choose the best word or phrase to complete each of these sentences.**

1 Corporate social .... traditionally had its own separate section in the annual financial report of large companies.

   a) reliability   b) reactivity   c) responsibility   d) reminder

2 The Prince of Wales's Sustainability project introduced the concept of a corporate reporting .... into companies' accounting systems which incorporated sustainability.

   a) procedure   b) system   c) process   d) framework

3 A company which is registered on a stock exchange is known as a .... company.

   a) listed   b) registered   c) liability   d) labelled

4 Before making an investment, it is wise to make a thorough investment ....

   a) research   b) test   c) study   d) analysis

5 Investment which takes the environment and society into consideration is called .... investment.

   a) sensitive   b) stable   c) substantial   d) sustainable

6 An investor who does not hold the main part of a company's shares is called a .... investor.

   a) small   b) minor   c) minority   d) insignificant

7 When a person or company borrows money and offers shares they own as collateral in case they cannot repay the loan, they .... their shares to the money lender.

   a) promise   b) agree   c) pledge   d) securitise

8 An independent agency that calculates the risk of investing in a company and gives it a rating based on this is called a(n) .... rating agency.

   a) investment   b) company   c) industrial   d) credit

9 A limited company whose shares are freely sold and traded, with a minimum share capital of £50,000 in the UK, is called a .... limited company.

   a) public   b) private   c) parent   d) property

10 When a company in financial difficulty is reorganised by an outside specialist with the aim of continuing some of its activities, this is known as ....

   a) reorganisation   b) liquidation   c) administration   d) bankruptcy

11 When a company stops operating because of financial difficulty and its assets are sold to pay its debts, this is called ....

   a) liquidity   b) bankruptcy   c) liquidation   d) closure

12 When banks borrow money in order to lend to customers, they obtain .... funding.

   a) credit   b) retail   c) wholesale   d) lent

13 A situation in which there is a short supply of money to lend to businesses and consumers is known as a credit ....

   a) loss   b) shortage   c) lack   d) crunch

14 A time when business activity increases rapidly is an economic ....

   a) boom   b) peak   c) cycle   d) bust

15 When a firm of auditors agrees that a company's accounts are true and fair, they sign them ....

   a) out   b) over   c) away   d) off

16 This is called giving it their .... approval.

   a) green light   b) good concern   c) going concern   d) green concern

17 If the auditors are dissatisfied with a company's accounts, they give an .... opinion.

   a) audit   b) average   c) adverse   d) awful

18 Auditors believe that they should not have complete liability in the event of failure of a client company due to fraud or negligence. They feel that .... limitation of their liability is fairer.

   a) partial   b) proportional   c) part   d) plain

19 The financial accounts of a group of companies is called the .... accounts.

   a) company   b) corporate   c) complete   d) consolidated

20 Auditors cannot look at every number in a company's accounts. Instead, they inspect a sample of figures. This is known as examining the company's accounts on a .... basis.

   a) trial   b) test   c) true   d) total

Answer key

Reading

A 1 F (*Most accountants work in-house for companies or organisations in the private, public or voluntary sectors.* (lines 5–7))
2 T (*... such as auditing, taxation, insolvency or forensic accounting.* (lines 10–12))
3 F (*... global accounting practices serving global clients ...* (lines 14–16))
4 T (*... accountancy training naturally tends to occur at a national level.* (lines 23–25))
5 F (*But accountancy training is not just about the initial qualification.* (lines 39–40))
6 F (*... including continuing professional education and lifelong learning.* (lines 45–46))
7 T (*Business and relationship skills have huge financial implications.* (lines 59–61), '*If you get training right, it can make a significant difference to competitive advantage ...*' (lines 80–82))

B 1 a competitive advantage (lines 51–52)
2 Proper training, experience and professional standards (lines 3–4)
3 Because taxation is a national issue (lines 20–23)
4 As 'the global organisation for the accountancy profession' (lines 32–34)
5 Strategic and managerial skills (lines 47–52)
6 Mobility (lines 67–69)
7 Lack of portability of national qualifications (lines 69–71)
8 Small or emerging markets that are growing rapidly (lines 84–86)
9 A common accounting language and set of standards and ethics (lines 92–95)
10 Inward investment and aid (lines 97–101)

Vocabulary

A 1 d 2 c 3 b 4 a
B 2 KPMG 3 KPMG 4 PwC 5 PwC 6 PwC 7 PwC
C 1 insolvency 2 relationship 3 team-management 4 auditing 5 forensic 6 employee appraisal
D 1 c 2 e 3 f 4 a 5 b 6 d
E **Contrast**
<u>Despite</u> the existence of global accounting practices serving global clients, the accountancy bodies that oversee training are almost entirely domestic ... (lines 14–18)
<u>Although</u> the widespread adoption of international accounting standards is making training easier, taxation is a national issue. (lines 20–23)
... global training at KPMG concentrates on values, skills and behaviours. <u>However</u>, KPMG's main strategic focus is the mobility ... (lines 65–68)
Similarity
The current trend is to emphasise strategy and management [...] <u>In this way</u>, at PricewaterhouseCoopers (PwC), the concept of the 'business adviser' ... (lines 47–55)
This includes skills such as managing teams [...] <u>Similarly</u>, global training at KPMG concentrates on ... (lines 57–66)
F 1 b 2 a 3 a

Reading

A 1 By developing partnerships with local institutes and an international reputation for the qualifications they offer. (lines 14–18)
2 It doesn't matter. (lines 25–26)
3 Language training (lines 39–40)
4 Finance processes are being outsourced to a variety of countries. (lines 43–47)
5 International Financial Reporting Standards (lines 53–56)
6 To help build a stronger economic system (lines 62–63)
7 Local control (lines 86–87)

B 1 Over half (lines 19–22)
2 The World Bank programme (lines 27–30)
3 Institute of Cost and Management Accountants of Bangladesh (lines 32–36)
4 Bangladesh (lines 49–50), Eastern Europe and central Asia (lines 64–65)
5 Academic, regulatory, government office (lines 56–58)
6 The building of strong national institutes (lines 77–78)
7 Chamber of auditors (lines 93–94)

C 1 local institutes 2 ACCA's 3 Bangladesh's 4 employers 5 International Financial Reporting Standards
6 Eastern Europe and Central Asia

Vocabulary

A 1 profession 2 a) bodies 2 b) institutes 3 International Financial Reporting Standards 4 regulator 5 government official 6 chamber

B 1 develop 2 development 3 Developing 4 developing 5 developing

C 1 International Financial Reporting Standards 2 accountancy profession 3 accountancy institutes 4 chamber of auditors 5 regulators 6 developing

D 1 b 2 d 3 a 4 e 5 f 6 c 7 g

E 1 b 2 b 3 a 4 a

UNIT 3

Reading

A 1 F ('*No one anticipated how big it was going to be!*' (lines 1–2))

2 T (*... they [CEOs] need to keep up to date ...* (lines 17–18))

3 F (*A changeover to IFRS involves far more changes [...] retraining staff and altering data-collection systems [...] changing pay policies and adjusting key accounting policies ...* (lines 22–27))

4 F (*Secondly, we had to understand how to produce the new style of accounts.* (lines 41–43))

5 F (*No two companies go through exactly the same experience ...* (lines 65–66))

6 T (*... different accounting rules in each country. Some of these were more geared towards tax collection ...* (lines 74–77))

B 1 *To take account of* (= to pay attention to) is a play on the word *accounting*.

2 anomalies in the reported accounts (lines 28–29)

3 They had to educate the market (investors/analysts) about what the different numbers in their financial statements meant. (lines 51–54)

4 Share price moves of 1 or 2 per cent (lines 56–59)

5 ... something that was promoted as only a change in bookkeeping ... (lines 61–63)

6 It was aimed at capital markets (investors). (lines 77–78)

7 The larger, more complex ones (lines 80–90)

Vocabulary

A 1 a) Chief Executive Officer b) bookkeepers c) Director of External Reporting

2 financial performance 3 a) reported accounts b) final financial statements 4 key accounting policies

5 anomalies 6 disclosure requirement 7 capital markets

B 1 adjustment 2 alter 3 changeover 4 conversion 5 reorientation 6 switch over

C 1 changeover/switchover 2 alter/change/adjust 3 key accounting policies 4 Director of External Reporting

5 reported accounts 6 disclosure requirements 7 anomalies

D 1 keep up to date with 2 understand 3 retrain 4 alter 5 change 6 adjust 7 produce 8 educate 9 prepare

E 1 b 2 a 3 a 4 a

UNIT 4

Reading 1

A 1 T (Total operating income)

2 T (Interest income, Interest expense, Net interest income)

3 F (Trading income was $3,274m lower in 2008 than in 2007.)

4 F (They are deducted from net operating income.)

5 F (It sold off some French ones.)

6 T (Tax expense)

7 T (Basic earning per ordinary share, Diluted earnings per ordinary share)

Vocabulary 1

A 1 b 2 f 3 c 4 a 5 d 6 e

Reading 2

A 1 T (Cash and balances at central banks)

2 T (Customer accounts)

3 F (Loans and advances to banks were $83,600m lower, and loans and advances to customers were $48,680 lower than in 2007.)

4 T (Derivatives)

5 T (Retirement benefit liabilities)

6 F (Total shareholders' equity was $34,569m lower in 2008 than in 2007.)

7 T (Goodwill and intangible assets)

8 T (Total equity and liabilities, Other reserves)

Vocabulary 2

A 1 assets   2 liabilities   3 loans   4 provisions   5 called-up share capital   6 equity   7 minority interests   8 reserves

Reading

A 1 F (*Pearson met or exceeded its previous guidance for 2008 in all its businesses, the publisher said this week.* (lines 1–3))

2 F (*... a number of 'bearish' announcements from rival educational, book and newspaper companies.* (lines 4–7))

3 F (*... rival educational, book and newspaper companies.* (lines 5–7))

4 T (*The owner of the* Financial Times ... (lines 7–8))

5 T (*Some of our markets will be tough this year ...* (lines 18–19))

6 T (*Simon Baker [...] commented, 'It is good news, but there are some question marks [...] people are generally going to be cautious about assuming all that will continue.' Alex de Groote [...] stated 'There are certainly no new horror stories, but I remain concerned about exposure to the education market in the US.* (lines 52–65))

7 T (*[Pearson's higher education business] has benefited from a contracting job market, which has encouraged more people to invest in continuing education rather than looking for employment.* (lines 69–73))

B 1 51p (line 13)   2 625p (line 28)   3 10–15% (line 35)   4 The strength of the dollar and a lower tax rate (lines 40–43)

5 Poor Christmas book sales and the impact of weak advertising market (lines 45–51)   6 20 per cent (line 77)

7 FT Publishing (lines 80–84)   8 Penguin Group UK (lines 86–91)

Vocabulary

A 1 bearish

2 1 growth   2 contracting   3 strength   4 weakness

B 1 around   2 about   3 approximately   4 slightly more than

C 1 guidance   2 trading update   3 resilience   4 late-cycle   5 counter-cyclical

D 1 a/b ii   2 c iv   3 d i   4 b/a iii

E 1 1 expected   2 could   3 will   4 might

2 1 could   2 might   3 expected   4 will

F 1 trading update; met   2 counter-cyclical; offset   3 growing   4 could; expected

5 around/about/approximately; slightly more than

Reading

A 1 T (*... the relaxing of fair-value accounting standards in late 2008 ...* (lines 2–4))

2 T (*European banks' accounting practices deteriorated as a result [...] according to Sir David Tweedie ...* (lines 1–4))

3 F (*He warned that any further interfering in accounting rules by politicians would risk destroying the long-running project towards developing a single global set of accounting rules.* (lines 10–14))

4 T (*The change helped troubled European banks reclassify some of their assets and avoid a hit to their earnings.* (lines 15–17))

5 F (*... the original 'fair-value' system ...* (line 48))

6 F (*... as markets plunged in 2008 ...* (lines 50–51))

7 T (*Sir David argued that it would be better if regulators changed the way they used a bank's accounts to calculate its capital needs.* (lines 79–82))

B 1 The IASB (International Accounting Standards Board) (lines 5–6)

2 The European Commission (lines 6–9)

3 More than €113bn (lines 17–19)

4 More than €3bn (lines 19–21)

5 The US (lines 31–36)

6 Disclose amortised cost valuations (lines 45–47)

7 That fair-value accounting was pro-cyclical because it helped to exaggerate the impact of a downturn and that their capital reserves were reduced because they had to report losses on assets which they continued to hold and had no intention of selling. (lines 64–72)

C 1 the banks'   2 the banks   3 the assets   4 the assets   5 the banks'   6 a bank's

Vocabulary

A 1 b i   2 a ii

B 1 adjustment   2 shift   3 assessment   4 watchdogs   5 capital needs

C 1 deteriorated   2 troubled   3 market volatility   4 reduced market value   5 disclose   6 write down   7 plunged   8 downturn

D 1 amortised cost   2 Watchdogs   3 plunge   4 market volatility   5 capital needs   6 write down

E 1 b   2 a   3 b   4 a   5 b   6 a   7 a   8 a

UNIT 7

Reading

A 1 Chinese regulatory reform, economic growth and entry to the World Trade Organisation (paragraph A)
2 Chemicals and automotive (paragraph B)
3 Outward (paragraph C)
4 Raw materials (paragraph E), global brands (paragraph F), skills (paragraph G)
5 Political opposition (paragraph F)
6 (Investment) banking (paragraph G)
7 These terms refer to merger and acquisition activity.

B 1 T (*China has become a key arena for global investment banks, keen to advise dynamic Chinese companies on mainland expansion opportunities.* (lines 9–13))
2 T (*Secondly, in sectors such as retail, existing Chinese companies are generally very small scale. This tends to make them less attractive to large foreign multinationals ...* (lines 34–39))
3 T (*China needed to sustain its breakneck economic growth, so it invested heavily in overseas iron ore, steel and coal mines.* (lines 43–46))
4 F (*In the future, private Chinese companies are likely to go for global brands ...* (lines 52–54))
5 T (*... relocating production to lower-cost mainland factories ...* (lines 54–55))
6 F (*Today, China has a high level of liquidity ...* (lines 64–65))
7 T (*... whereas several years ago, Chinese lenders were largely broke.* (lines 67–69))
8 T (*At that time, Beijing permitted foreign investors to spend a combined $20bn to acquire stakes in domestic lenders in return for help to improve risk management.* (lines 69–73))

C 1 China's   2 investment banks advising Chinese companies on their overseas mergers-and-acquisitions strategy
3 Lenovo   4 several years ago   5 China   6 domestic M&A

Vocabulary

A 1 b   2 a   3 e   4 f   5 d   6 c
B 1 d   2 e   3 h   4 f   5 g   6 a   7 b   8 i   9 c
C 1 investment bank   2 merger   3 acquisition   4 inbound   5 entrepreneur   6 outbound
D 1 mergers; acquisitions   2 global brands   3 Corporate financiers   4 risk-management   5 Regulatory reform
6 foreign investment   7 scale   8 broke   9 hostile bid
E 1 up; for   2 in   3 to   4 on   5 in   6 out; to

UNIT 8

Reading

A 1 b   2 b   3 c   4 b
B 1 E   2 A   3 D   4 C   5 B
C 1 T (*Debt finance, such as a bank loan, is generally much more readily available [...] is lower ...* (lines 7–14))
2 T (*... the business in question already exists, and its trading history can be analysed.* (lines 15–17)
3 F (*Although these companies are still put in the high-risk category, ...* (lines 30–32))
4 F (*The return they ask for mainly depends on the amount of risk the investment presents: the greater the risk, the greater the required reward.* (lines 42–46))
5 F (*This shows the return in terms of the annual percentage of return the investor is likely to get over the lifetime of the investment.* (lines 48–51))
6 F (*They know that most of the companies will fail completely, some will succeed, but only a few will be very successful.* (lines 60–63))

Vocabulary

A 1 a) company   b) entrepreneur   c) capital
2 a) people   b) technical   c) market
3 a) debt finance   b) investment capital
B 1 high-risk   2 management buyout   3 fast-growth   4 innovation company   5 internal rate of return
6 business plan   7 portfolio of investments   8 high return
C 1 investor   2 return   3 venture   4 IRR   5 fund   6 fail   7 worth
D 1 a   2 b   3 a   4 a   5 a
E 1 start-up; investments   2 internal rate; return   3 cover   4 start-up companies; magnitude
5 business plan; investment   6 fast-growth curve   7 worth   8 high return

Before you read

3   It refers to Posh Spice, a member of the all-girl pop group The Spice Girls. Her real name is Victoria Beckham and she is the wife of footballer David Beckham. The pun relates to her luxury image and lifestyle.

Reading

A   1 F (*Daimler's very poor results yesterday show that even luxury car makers are running out of fuel.* (lines 1–3))
2 F (*But this way lies danger.* (line 11))
3 T (*Porsche's slowly-slowly takeover of Volkswagen (VW), via cash-settled call options, has so far proved extremely profitable.* (lines 20–23))
4 T (*This helped it make a cool €6.8bn profit from options trades in that year, whereas it made only €1bn from selling cars.* (lines 27–31))
5 F (*... a German law, which currently allows the State of Lower Saxony to exercise a blocking minority via its 20-per-cent stake in VW ...* (lines 37–40))
6 T (*If the European Commission legal challenge were unsuccessful, and Porsche decided not to buy the remaining amount of shares to take its stake to 75 per cent, so closed its options position, VW's free float would increase and the price of its shares would consequently fall.* (lines 58–65))
7 F (*Porsche says it values VW at €117 a share [...] HSBC, however, estimates fair value of VW's shares at a much more conservative €74 ...* (lines 66–71))

B   1 Schaeffler and Merckle   2 €6.8bn   3 €1bn   4 75%   5 The State of Lower Saxony; 20% (a blocking minority)
6 By a legal challenge to the European Commission   7 €10bn; to finance the rest of the takeover

Vocabulary

A   1 financial engineering   2 highly leveraged   3 collateral   4 cash-settled   5 blocking minority   6 exposure
7 a) short squeeze b) share shortage   8 free float

B   1 e   2 a   3 c   4 f   5 b   6 d

C   1 e i   2 a v   3 d ii   4 f iii   5 b vi   6 c iv

D   1 derivatives   2 options   3 blocking minority   4 share shortage/short squeeze 5 close; position; free float
6 write; down   7 financial engineering

Before you read

1 Financial items   2 Environmental issues, people issues   3 Bean counters   4 Environmental (sustainability) issues

Reading

A   1 They didn't have figures to measure.
2 He wanted to radically transform their business culture.
3 The Prince of Wales's Accounting for Sustainability Project
4 The 'connected reporting framework'
5 To link sustainability measures to the main financial report so that they have a direct impact on corporate strategy.
6 A success. The connection of the two disciplines produced strategic and financial change.
7 It translated into significant savings and moved sustainability onto senior executives' agendas.
8 If you show how sustainability links with strategy, it becomes more fundamental to running the business.

B   1 They set a target to reduce carbon emissions from their energy generation activities by 60 per cent by 2020. (lines 20–23)
2 The finance department (lines 46–47)
3 Polluting emissions, waste and usage of water, energy and other finite resources (lines 50–52)
4 No, also the public sector (lines 79–80)
5 Graduate recruits and customers (lines 86–90)

Vocabulary

A   1 green   2 corporate social responsibility   3 sustainability   4 accounting for sustainability   5 framework
6 strategic

B   1 sustain   2 sustainable/sustained   3 measure   4 measurement   5 transform   6 transformable/transformed
7 connectable/connected   8 connection   9 isolate   10 isolation   11 reduced   12 reduction   13 aligned
14 alignment   15 pioneering   16 pioneer

C   1 c   2 g   3 d   4 i   5 a   6 e   7 b   8 h   9 f   10 j

D 1 Sustainability   2 embedded   3 corporate social responsibility   4 connected reporting   5 strategic
6 performance driver   7 green
E To produce (lines 54–55); to bring about (line 61); to translate into (line 64)
F 1 b   2 b   3 a   4 b   5 b   6 a

UNIT 11

Reading

A 1 Financial factors such as how the company's current share price relates to the fair value of the stock
2 A sustainable investment process including corporate responsibility and human rights issues
3 It improves risk management.
4 By being careful about the long-term impact of your behaviour, you invest in ways which don't undermine the financial system.
5 Equities
6 This involves saving energy, which in turn saves costs.
7 Adding value to projects, rather than simply engaging in price speculation
8 Whether it is possible to take the environment into account and make a profit in difficult markets.
B 1 The CFA Institute Centre for Financial Market Integrity (lines 28–31)
2 Oxfam (line 42), Hermes Equity Ownership Services (line 53), Oxford Group (line 65)
3 Responsible investors benefit from better risk management, greater transparency, and an active engagement with companies to promote better management. (lines 35–39)
4 Renewable energy (line 68)
5 Areas designated as regeneration targets (lines 74–80)
6 A sustainable supply chain (line 78)
C 3, 5, 8 and 9 are used to express contrast.

Vocabulary

A 1 1 sustainable (line 8)   2 analysis (line 41)   3 behaviour (line 50)   4 real-estate (line 59)   5 opportunity (line 93)
2 1 asset managers   2 risk management   3 framework   4 listed   5 renewable energy   6 adding value
7 price speculation
B 1 c   2 f   3 a   4 g   5 b   6 d   7 e   8 j   9 i   10 h
C 1 framework   2 risk management   3 listed   4 real estate   5 price speculation
6 investment analysis   7 add; value   8 sustainable supply
D 1 a   2 a   3 b   4 b   5 a   6 b   7 a   8 b

UNIT 12

Reading

A 1 F (… *India's fourth-largest information technology group* … (lines 3–4))
2 T (… *India's fourth-largest information technology group by revenue* … (lines 3–4))
3 F (… *this fraud* … (line 21))
4 F (… *which raised questions over just how the company's auditor, PwC, and stock-market regulators had failed to spot it.* (lines 33–36))
5 F (*He had pledged his family's 8-per-cent stake in Satyam to lenders.* (lines 53–54))
6 F (*What these investors didn't know was that Mr Raju was sitting on a time bomb.* (lines 51–53))
7 T (*The lenders had sold almost all of the Raju family's shares and, as a result, the company's share price had plummeted to a fraction of its former value.* (lines 60–64))
8 T (… *two weeks after the confession, the Securities and Exchange Board of India (SEBI), the stock-market regulator, made it mandatory for controlling shareholders to declare their share pledges.* (lines 83–88))
B 1 effect   2 cause   3 cause   4 effect   5 effect
C 1 Information technology   2 Sensex Index   3 To cover up the scandal   4 They are controlled by families.
5 The Securities and Exchange Board of India (SEBI)

Vocabulary

A 1 Chairman   2 Board of Directors   3 scam   4 independent directors   5 institutional investors
6 controlling shareholders   7 minority investors   8 corporate disclosure requirements   9 stock-market regulator
B 1 1 B   2 B   3 C   4 A   5 A   6 C   7 A   8 B   9 A   10 C   11 A   12 B   13 B   14 C   15 A
2 1 borrow   2 security   3 pledge   4 lender
3 1 share broker   2 minimum margin   3 on margin   4 margin call
C 1 Board of Directors   2 stock-market regulator   3 As a result; corporate disclosure   4 Minority investors
5 pledged; security   6 plummet/crash/dive/drop/fall; margin call
D 1 a   2 b   3 a   4 a   5 b   6 b   7 a   8 a

UNIT 13

Reading

A 1 1 F (*The Northern Rock Building Society converted into a public limited company in 1997.* (paragraph A))
2 T (*... one of the largest mortgage lenders in the UK ...* (paragraph A))
3 T (*... the bank was forced to borrow emergency money from the Bank of England.* (paragraph B))
4 T (*... many withdrew their savings in the first run on a bank in Britain for around 140 years.* (paragraph B))
5 F (*'You all failed' [...] banks, central banks and regulators all faced criticism ...* (lines 3–10))
6 T (*Corporate credit-rating agencies assess the creditworthiness of bonds and bond issuers.* (lines 19–21))
7 F (*Furthermore, S&P pointed out that it had reported the 'possible risk' for investors of 'creative financing opportunities within the residential mortgage realm' as early as April 2005.* (lines 76–80))

B 1 1997–2007   2 The subprime crisis   3 Fitch, Moody's and Standard & Poor's (S&P)
4 Triple-A (AAA/Aaa) / investment grade   5 C/D / junk bond   6 The companies whose products they rate
7 There should be more choice.   8 International Organisation of Securities Commissions (IOSCO)

Vocabulary

A 1 a   2 f   3 e   4 c   5 b   6 d   7 h   8 g
B 1 as risky as   2 slightly riskier than   3 the safest   4 considerably safer than   5 the riskiest / in default
6 as safe as   7 much riskier than
C 1 c   2 a   3 d   4 b   5 f   6 e
D 1 1 bank   2 lender   3 borrower   4 repayments   5 bond   6 investor   7 interest   8 securitised
2 1 treasury committee   2 credit-rating   3 investment-grade   4 highest risk   5 subprime mortgages
6 bond issuers   7 securities regulator

UNIT 14

Reading

A 1 A small retail business
2 There has been a downturn in trading.
3 His responsibilities and financial liabilities
4 The company's directors
5 The company's creditors
6 An insolvency practitioner
7 Its assets
8 They should hold regular meetings.

B 1 Personal liability for debts, disqualification as company director, imprisonment (lines 18–22)
2 Constitution (articles) of the company, the Companies Act (lines 29–30)
3 Up-to-date statutory accounts, management accounts, forecasts based on latest order book. (lines 40–43)
4 Themselves (lines 49–51)
5 Sell assets at low value, take on new supplies or lines of credit (lines 53–58)
6 Specific creditors (lines 63–65)
7 Keep minutes of discussions and decisions, detail circumstances that justify continued trading (lines 66–72)

Vocabulary

A 1 1 c   2 d   3 a   4 b
2 1 b   2 c   3 e   4 a   5 f   6 d   7 h   8 g
B 1 b   2 g   3 c   4 e   5 d   6 h   7 a   8 f
C 1 sharp downturn   2 insolvent   3 liquidation   4 fraudulent   5 remedies   6 disqualification   7 minutes
8 order book
D 1 a   2 a   3 b   4 a   5 a   6 b

UNIT 15

Reading

A 1 The bank appeared to be very successful at that time.
2 The bank nearly collapsed. (It was rescued by another bank and the British tax payer.)
3 Head of Regulatory Risk
4 He said its growth strategy was too fast and that it risked its financial stability. He thought the bank was taking too many risks.
5 A supermarket.
6 Analysts
7 An economic slowdown

B 1 Chief Executive Officer (CEO) (line 1)
2 Deputy Chairman of the Financial Services Authority (lines 22–23)

3 Halifax and Bank of Scotland (lines 32–33)
4 Halifax relied more heavily on retail (savers') deposits; Bank of Scotland borrowed more of its money from the wholesale markets. (lines 35–40)
5 His warnings were not allowed to be put in the official minutes of the meeting by the bank's CFO. (lines 59–63)
6 Retail and real-estate entrepreneurs (lines 71–72)
7 The bank was overexposed to it. (lines 89–91)

C 1 That Crosby already understood the mistakes made and the danger the bank was in.
2 Risk management.
3 *Bet* normally relates to gambling. It suggests that the bank had a risk-taking approach to business.
4 HBOS has grown its [corporate] loan book significantly faster than other large banks. (lines 77–80)

Vocabulary

A 1 b 2 d 3 a 4 f 5 c 6 e
B 1 (lines 6–7), 4 (lines 7–8), 6 (lines 14–15), 8 (line 48), 10 (line 69)
C 1 g 2 c 3 f 4 h 5 a 6 b 7 d 8 e
D 1 credit crunch 2 hit; peak; point; collapse 3 vulnerable 4 wholesale funding; retail
5 loan exposure 6 boom; recession
E 1 a 2 a 3 b 4 b

UNIT 16

Reading

A 1 F (*Most years, the auditor's report [...] attracts little interest.* (lines 11–16))
2 T (*At worst, auditors can give an 'adverse opinion', indicating a general and serious disagreement with the directors' statement of the company's financial position.* (lines 23–27))
3 T (*In volatile markets, however, even a 'qualified opinion', indicating a limited and specific concern, can act as a death warning.* (lines 27–30) *There is a danger that the market will react to this and it will become a self-fulfilling prophecy ...* (lines 53–55))
4 F (*After the failure of many dotcom companies in 2001, a wave of lawsuits against audit firms followed.* (lines 59–62))
5 T (*Since then, regulators have made it clear they will take a firm line with audit firms.* (lines 62–64))
6 T (*So in a difficult year, auditors are even more rigorous than usual.* (lines 85–87))

B 1 31 December 2 A year 3 Adverse opinion 4 Going-concern approval 5 Emphasis of matter paragraph
6 Significant level of concern, material uncertainty 7 Dotcom failures

Vocabulary

A 1 jargon 2 jittery 3 standardised 4 signed off 5 disclosure(s) 6 dotcom 7 lawsuit 8 clean opinion
9 bank facility 10 bank mandate
B 1 b 2 d 3 a 4 c
C 1 going-concern 2 signed off 3 bank facility 4 disclosure; emphasis of matter 5 adverse opinion
D 1 a 2 b 3 b 4 a 5 a 6 b

UNIT 17

Reading

A 1 T (*Now, the latest attempt to allow UK audit firms to agree specific limits on their liability ...* (lines 5–7))
2 F (*But every time a possible solution to the auditors' problem had been found, it had eventually been rejected.* (lines 2–5))
3 F (*... was in the hands of a US regulator.* (line 8))
4 F (*It was at this point that the SEC arrived on the scene [...] and objected that this would not be in investors' interests.* (lines 79–87) *Everything was on hold once again.* (lines 93–94))

B a 3 b 6 c 5 d 1 e 8 f 9 g 2 h 7 i 4

C 1 When UK companies are listed in the US or have raised money in US markets.
2 Because they thought it was dishonest and not sustainable, as auditors do not have unlimited funds.
3 The United States
4 No, it would be done on a contractual basis, company by company, and each board of directors would have to vote at the annual shareholders' meeting.
5 Shareholders' interests
6 The Institute of Chartered Accountants of England & Wales (ICAEW) and the Financial Reporting Council (FRC)
7 It saw the possibility of conspiracies between auditors and directors and objected that this would not be in investors' interests.

Vocabulary

A 1 solve 2 rejection 3 achievement 4 objection 5 limit 6 implement 7 propose 8 oppose

B 1 b 2 d 3 a 4 f 5 c 6 e 7 h 8 g

C 1 b 2 b 3 a 4 b 5 b 6 a 7 b

D 1 limitation 2 liability 3 sole financial responsibility 4 resolution 5 contractual basis 6 legal debate
7 legal opinion 8 jurisdiction

E 1 was in the hands of 2 were seen as having very deep pockets 3 it was not sustainable 4 with many setbacks
5 to cap their liability 6 cosy deal

UNIT 18

Reading

A 1 F (*... year ended 31 March 2008 [...] which comprise the balance sheet ...* (lines 2–3))
2 F (*... in accordance with relevant legal and regulatory requirements and International Standards on Auditing
(UK and Ireland).* (lines 18–20))
3 T (*We report to you our opinion as to whether the parent Company Financial Statements give a true and fair view ...*
(lines 21–22))
4 F (*... in accordance with the Companies Act 1985.* (lines 24–25))
5 T (*We also report to you whether in our opinion the Directors' Report is consistent with the parent Company
Financial Statements.* (lines 25–27))
6 T (*Our responsibility does not extend to any further information outside the annual report.* (lines 40–41))

B 1 Parent Company Financial Statements and Consolidated Financial Statements
2 In notes 1 to 10 in the parent Company Financial Statements.
3 a) If the parent Company Financial Statements didn't give a true and fair view.
b) If the parent Company Financial Statements hadn't been properly prepared in accordance with the Companies Act 1985.
c) If Directors' Report wasn't consistent with the parent Company Financial Statements.
4 a) If the Company has not kept proper accounting records.
b) If the auditors have not received all the information and explanations hey require for their audit.
c) If information specified by law regarding directors' remuneration and other transactions is not disclosed.
5 The Auditing Practices Board
6 Yes 7 Yes 8 Yes

C 1 c 2 b 3 d 4 a

Vocabulary

A 1 for the year ended 2 consolidated 3 directors' remuneration report
4 Statement of Directors' Responsibilities 5 specified by law 6 misstatements 7 material inconsistencies
8 test basis 9 estimates and judgements 10 reasonable assurance

B 1 b 2 a 3 c

C 1 b 2 d 3 e 4 a 5 c 6 f

D 1 for the year ended 2 comprises 3 set out 4 in accordance with 5 consistent with 6 test basis
7 estimates and judgements 8 appropriate 9 so as to 10 reasonable assurance 11 inconsistencies
12 misstatements

CHECK TEST 1

A 1 insolvency 2 forensic 3 International Financial Reporting Standards 4 key accounting policies 5 loan
6 Reserves 7 Depreciation 8 Dividend 9 Goodwill 10 counter-cyclical 11 late-cycle
12 International Accounting Standards Board 13 hostile 14 financiers 15 entrepreneur 16 capital
17 rate of return 18 financial engineering 19 collateral 20 liquidity

B 1 b 2 c 3 a 4 d 5 b 6 d 7 b 8 c 9 a 10 d 11 b 12 c 13 d 14 c 15 d 16 d
17 b 18 c 19 a 20 b

CHECK TEST 2

A 1 sustainability 2 fully embedded 3 strategic 4 performance 5 speculation 6 supply 7 institutional
8 disclosure 9 margin 10 central 11 subprime 12 receivership 13 fraudulent 14 deposits
15 recession 16 lawsuit 17 bank mandate 18 jurisdiction 19 misstatement 20 material inconsistencies

B 1 c 2 d 3 a 4 d 5 d 6 c 7 c 8 d 9 a 10 c 11 c 12 c 13 d 14 a 15 d 16 c 17 c 18 b
19 d 20 b

Glossary

A

accountancy *n.* the profession or work done by accountants in keeping the financial records of organisations and in giving advice to clients on tax and other financial matters

accountancy firm *n.* a group of accountants who have entered into partnership with one another to provide accounting and auditing services for a fee

accountancy partner *n.* an individual accountant who belongs to an accountancy partnership

accountant *n.* a professional person whose job it is to keep and check the financial records of an organisation, or to advise clients on tax and other financial matters

accounting rule/standard *n.* an official instruction on how something must be treated and presented in accounts

accounting system *n.* the rules used for accounting in a particular company or place

accounts *n.pl.* the complete set of records showing money coming into and going out of a business, its profits and its financial situation

acquisition *n.* **1** when one company buys another one, or part of another one **2** a company or part of a company that is bought by another company

add-on *n.* one thing added as a supplement to another

administration *n.* (UK) when a company in financial difficulty is reorganised by an outside specialist with the aim of continuing some of its activities so that it can avoid liquidation

administrative expenses *n.pl.* expenses relating to the managerial and general administrative activities of a business rather than those relating to the manufacture and sale of goods

adverse opinion *n.* a statement in the auditor's report of a company's annual accounts indicating a large enough disagreement with the company's view of its activities and finances that the auditor considers the accounts misleading

agenda *n.* **1** a list of the subjects to be discussed at a meeting **2** a list of things that someone considers important or that they are planning to do

amortised cost valuation *n.* when an asset's market value at any specific point in time is not taken into account and the asset value is assumed to increase steadily over the asset's lifetime

analyst *n.* someone who is a specialist in a particular subject, market or industry and examines information relating to it in order to give their views about what will happen or should be done

annual general meeting *n.* an official yearly meeting of the shareholders and directors of a company, at which the company's accounts are presented, the auditors are chosen, and the amount of dividend is decided, as required by law

annual report *n.* a report presented each year by the directors of a company to the members and shareholders, containing financial information about the company's trading activities and the documents the company must produce by law, which are the balance sheet, the profit and loss account, and the auditor's and directors' reports

anomaly *n.* something that is noticeable because it is different from what is usual

assessment *n.* a judgement that you make about a person or situation after considering all the information

asset *n.* something belonging to an individual or a business that has value or the power to earn money

asset manager *n.* a person who looks after someone else's money, investments in stocks and shares, etc.

association *n.* an organised body of people who have an interest, activity or purpose in common; a society

audit report *n.* an official document written by an auditor, stating whether the accounts that have been examined have been kept properly and if there is anything the auditor is not happy with

auditing *n.* **1** an official examination of a person's or organisation's accounts by an expert, to check that they are true and honest **2** an examination of an organisation's activities or performance

auditing standards *n.pl.* a set of systematic guidelines used by auditors when conducting audits on companies' finances, ensuring the accuracy, consistency and verifiability of auditors' actions and reports

auditor *n.* an outside specialist accountant that checks that an individual's or organisation's accounts are true and honest

B

balance sheet *n.* a document showing a company's financial position and wealth at a particular time, often the last day of its financial year

bank facility *n.* an arrangement made by a bank for its customers which lets them use its services, for example borrowing and investing

bank loan *n.* an amount of money lent by a bank

bank mandate *n.* a written instruction to a bank, asking it to make regular payments or to open a new account.

banking sector *n.* the part of the economy made up by banks

behaviours *n.pl.* the ways that someone or something acts in different situations

blocking minority *n.* If someone has a *blocking minority*, they own a large number of shares in a company, and they therefore have the power to prevent other companies from buying or taking control of it.

board of directors *n.* the group of people who have been elected to manage a company by those holding shares in the company

body *n.* a collective group with a common interest

bond issuer *n.* a company or municipality offering securities for sale to investors

bookkeeper *n.* a person whose job it is to keep an official record of all the money received into and paid out of a business

boom *n.* a time when business activity increases rapidly so that the demand for goods increases, wages go up and unemployment falls

brand *n.* a name given to a product by a company so that the product can easily be recognised by its name or its design

building society *n.* an organisation providing financial services to customers, especially lending money in the form of mortgages to buy a house or flat and paying interest to savers.

business adviser *n.* an expert who gives information to someone so that they are able to make a good business decision

business culture *n.* the ideas and beliefs that are shared by a particular group of people in a particular organisation

business empire *n.* a group of companies or organisations controlled by one powerful company or individuals

business plan *n.* a document produced by a company, especially a new company, giving details of expected sales and costs, and how the business can be financed, and showing why the plan will make money

C

call option *n.* an option that gives you the right to buy shares at a particular price in the future. Investors who buy *call options* think the market will rise above that price.

capital needs *n.pl.* the amount of cash and easily liquidated assets that a bank or broker/dealer needs to meet stock-exchange regulations, usually expressed as a proportion of total liabilities

central bank *n.* the official bank of a country, which is responsible for setting interest rates, controlling the money supply, producing banknotes and making money available, and keeping the country's supply of foreign currency and gold, etc.

chamber of auditors *n.* a self-governing professional organisation for the purpose of regulation of the audit profession

changeover *n.* a change from one system or way of doing something to another

Chief Executive Officer (CEO) *n.* the manager with the most authority in the normal, everyday management of a company. The job of *Chief Executive Officer* is sometimes combined with other jobs, such as that of president.

clean opinion *n.* a good report that is given about a company's finances by an auditor who has officially checked them

collateral *n.* assets promised by a borrower to a lender if the borrower cannot repay a loan

Companies Act (2006) *n.* an Act of Parliament of the United Kingdom of Great Britain and Northern Ireland which regulates companies within that jurisdiction and replaces the 1985 Act

competitive advantage *n.* an advantage that makes a company more able to succeed in competing with others

competitor *n.* a person, product, company or country that is competing with another

conflict of interest *n.* a situation in which you cannot do your job fairly because you have the power to decide something in a way that would be to your advantage, although this may not be the best decision

connected reporting framework *n.* a reporting model for companies and organisations which presents key information about sustainability along with the usual financial information

consolidated financial statement *n.* accounts showing the combined trading results and financial position of a group of companies

conspiracy *n.* a secret plan that is made by two or more people to do something harmful or illegal

constitution *n.* the system of rules and principles that an organisation must follow

consultation document *n.* a document which sets out various ideas on which people can give their opinions before a decision is made

contents section *n.* a list found at the beginning of a document or book that lists the different items that can be found in it

controlling shareholder *n.* someone who owns more than half the shares in a company

conversion *n.* when something changes from being one thing to being another, for example when a building society becomes a bank

corporate bond *n.* a tradable IOU (I owe you). Companies and other organisations issue *bonds* to raise money; they must repay the bondholder according to specific terms. *Bonds* can be traded on established markets. In most cases, a *bond* is repaid at its original value on a particular date, and has a fixed rate of interest that is paid at regular intervals until it is repaid.

corporate disclosure requirement *n.* the duty of a company or organisation to inform customers and shareholders about facts that will influence their decision-making

corporate failure *n.* when a business that is not successful has to close because it is losing money

corporate financier *n.* a person or organisation that provides money for investment

corporate governance *n.* the way a company is managed at the highest level

corporate social responsibility (CSR) *n.* the idea that a company's role is not just about producing goods, but that it has a duty to help people in society and protect the environment

corporate strategy *n.* the way a company decides to act in the future, based on an analysis of factors such as the markets it operates in, its competitors and customers and its workforce

counter party *n.* the person or company who you are buying from or selling to

counter-cyclical *adj.* not following the normal pattern of business activity, for example increasing when other activities are decreasing

creative financing *n.* unusual but not illegal ways of getting or providing finance

credit crunch *n.* when borrowing money becomes difficult because banks are forced to reduce the amount they lend

credit-rating agency *n.* an agency which gives information about the financial strength of companies and governments to financial institutions and suppliers so that they can decide whether to lend money or allow goods to be bought on credit

credit squeeze *n.* a period of time when the government strictly limits the amount of lending that banks are allowed to do, leading to businesses and individuals having difficulty getting loans and paying more interest on them

creditor *n.* a person or business to whom another person or business owes money

creditworthy *adj.* If a country, business or individual is *creditworthy*, they are in a good position financially and have a good record of paying back loans on time, so institutions can lend money to them with confidence that the money will be paid back.

D

debt *n.* money that a person, organisation or country owes to another

depreciation *n.* the gradual loss in value of a fixed asset that wears out over a number of years or needs to be replaced regularly. Under tax law, the amount lost each year can be taken away from a business's profits, reducing the amount of tax to be paid.

derivative *n.* something such as an option or future

derivatives position *n.* when you hold a derivative product such as an option

developing nation *n.* a country that is changing its economy from one based mainly on farming to one based on industry

directors' remuneration report *n.* a report which states on which basis a company's directors have been rewarded

directors' report *n.* a statement by a company's directors in its annual accounts giving the directors' opinion of the state of the company, and how much should be paid to people owing shares in the company

disqualification *n.* when someone is stopped from taking part in an activity (such as being a company director) because they have broken a rule

dividend *n.* a part of the profits of a company for a particular period of time that is paid to shareholders for each share that they own

domestic market *n.* the country you live in or where a company is based, seen as a place where goods or services can be sold

dotcom *n.* a company that does business using the Internet or provides a service on the Internet

E

earnings *n.pl.* the profit that a company makes in a particular period of time, or the total profits that companies make in a particular industry or economy in a particular period of time

earnings per share *n.pl.* a company's profits for a period of time divided by the number of its shares

economic downturn *n.* the part of the economic cycle when prices or the value of stocks and shares fall and unemployment rises

economic growth *n.* an increase in the value of goods and services produced in a country or area

economic slowdown *n.* see **economic downturn**

economic system *n.* the particular way in which the economy of a country is organised, for example whether the economy is controlled by the government or allowed to develop in its own way

economy *n.* the system by which a country's goods and services are produced and used, or a country considered in this way

emerging market *n.* a market, especially in Asia, Africa and South America, that is just starting to have influence or power in trade

emphasis-of-matter paragraph *n.* an optional paragraph in an auditor's report that is used if the auditor considers that information is adequately disclosed in the financial statements, but that the reader's attention should be drawn to important matters in the notes

entrepreneur *n.* someone who starts a company and takes risks in order to make a profit

ESG factors *n.pl.* factors relating to the way a company is managed at the highest level and the way it takes care of the environment and the people who are connected to it

equities *n.pl.* trading in companies' shares on a stock market, rather than trading on other types of market

equity *n.* the capital that a company has from shares rather than from loans

equity fund *n.* a fund that invests in company shares

ESG framework *n.* a system which helps companies to take environmental, social and governance factors into account when decision-making and accounting for what they do

estimate *n.* a calculation of what the value, size, amount, etc. of something will probably be

ethics *n.pl.* moral rules or principles of behaviour that should guide members of a profession or organisation and make them deal honestly and fairly with each other and with their customers

evidence *n.* **1** information or facts given in a court of law to prove that someone is guilty **2** something which is clearly visible to everybody

expansion *n.* when something, such as a company, industry or economy increases or is increased in size, amount or number

expense *n.* an amount of money that a business or organisation has to spend on something

exposure *n.* the amount of money that a bank lends to a customer or an investor invests, which they risk losing if the customer does not repay the loan or the investor's investments do badly, for example on the stock market

external reporting *n.* the reporting of a company's activities and financial results to the outside world, such as customers, suppliers and investors

F

fair-value accounting *n.* when an asset's valuation at any specific point in time is based on the amount of money that could be obtained if the asset were sold at that time

fee *n.* an amount of money paid to a professional person or organisation for their services

finance *n.* money provided or lent, for example by a bank for investment or consumption

finance director *n.* someone who is in charge of the financial activities of a company

finance function *n.* the department that deals with the financial activities of a company

financial analysis *n.* analysis of the financial state of a company or potential investment

financial engineering *n.* arranging finances and investments in a clever, profitable and sometimes slightly dishonest way

financial instrument *n.* an investment such as a bond or share

financial investment *n.* putting money into a business or other investment with the aim of making a profit

financial liability *n.* the amount of money which a director of a business which is becoming insolvent would owe to the business's creditors

financial performance *n.* the degree to which a company, investment or financial market is profitable

financial reporting system *n.* part of a company's management information system that processes financial transactions to provide internal reporting to managers for use in planning and controlling current and future operations and for external reporting

financial return *n.* the profit made from an investment

financial services *n.pl.* the business activity of giving advice about investments and selling investments to people and organisations

financial statement *n.* a statement showing the financial state of a business, at the end of a particular period of time, including its balance sheet, profit and loss account and other necessary information

financing facility *n.* a loan or overdraft which a bank has agreed to give a company or individual

forecast *n.* a description of what is likely to happen in the future, based on information that is available now

foreign investment *n.* investment in a country other than your own

forensic accounting *n.* when a company's financial records are officially checked in order to find out if there has been any illegal activity

framework *n.* a set of ideas, rules or beliefs from which something is developed, or on which decisions are based

fraud *n.* a method of illegally getting money from a person or organisation, often using clever and complicated methods

fraudulent trading *n.* carrying out business activities using business documents, etc. which are intended to deceive

free float *n.* the number of shares of a particular company which exceed the number in demand

fund *n.* a company whose activity is putting money from investors into a particular type of investment or a range of investments, or an amount of money invested in this way, an amount of money that is obtained and used for a particular purpose

fund manager *n.* someone whose job is to manage a particular type of investment for a financial institution or its clients

funding model *n.* a particular way of funding something

future *n.* an agreement to buy or sell something such as a particular product or raw material, currency or security on a fixed date in the future at a fixed price

G

gain *n.* an increase in value or amount

GAAP *n.* Generally Accepted Accounting Practice

going concern *n.* a business which is considered able to continue operating in the foreseeable future, necessary in order to get credit and finance from suppliers and banks

going-concern approval *n.* when an independent auditor confirms in their auditor's report that a business is a going concern

goodwill *n.* the value that a business has in addition to the value of its assets. *Goodwill* includes things such as the good reputation that a business has, the names of its products, and the good relations it has with its customers.

government official *n.* someone who holds a responsible position in a government organisation

grading system *n.* the way the size or quality of something is officially assessed

growth curve *n.* a diagram showing how much a price or amount grows over time

guidance *n.* information about the company's outlook and earnings which is often used by analysts and investors as a guide to that company's future performance

H

holding *n.* **1** an amount of a particular type of investment owned by a person or organisation **2** a quantity of shares held in a company by a particular shareholder

I

implementation *n.* when you take action or make changes that you have officially decided should happen

imprisonment *n.* the state of being in prison, or the time someone spends there

income statement *n.* a statement showing the amount of money earned and spent in a particular period of time by a company

independent director *n.* a non-executive director who does not form part of the executive management team and is not an employee of the company

information system *n.* a computer system used to communicate information in an organisation, for example an intranet

information technology *n.* the study or use of electronic processes for storing information and making it available

infrastructure *n.* **1** the basic systems and structures that a country needs to make economic activity possible, for example transport, communications and power supplies **2** the basic systems and equipment needed for an industry or business to operate successfully

innovation *n.* a new idea, method or invention the introduction of new ideas or methods

insolvency *n.* a situation in which a person or a company does not have enough money or assets to pay their debts

insolvency practitioner *n.* (UK) a person or organisation that can, by law, act for a company that is declaring itself to be insolvent

institutional investor *n.* a financial institution such as a bank or insurance company that invests in something

intangible asset *n.* something that a business has and can make money from, but that is not something physical and so cannot easily be valued, for example a name of a product, technical knowledge, loyalty from customers

interest *n.* an amount paid by a borrower to a lender, in addition to the repayment of the original capital, or by a bank to a depositor (i.e. someone keeping money in an account there)

internal rate of return *n.* a measure of the value of an investment, expressed as a percentage and calculated by comparing the profit in a year with the amount that was originally invested

International Accounting Standards (IAS) *n.pl.* standards for the preparation and presentation of financial statements created by the International Accounting Standards Committee (IASC). The International Accounting Standards Board (IASB) took over the designing of these in 2001.

investment *n.* **1** when money is put into a business, or the money which is put into the business, with the aim of making a profit **2** something you buy, such as shares, bonds or property, in order to make a profit

investment analysis *n.* assessment of economic and market trends, earnings and other indicators and factors to determine suitable investment strategies

investment bank *n.* a bank that buys stocks and shares and then sells them to members of the public. *Investment banks* also offer advice on things such as mergers and takeovers.

investment behaviour *n.* the way that investors make different investment decisions in different situations

investment capital *n.* money which is invested in a company in order to produce a return or profit

investment opportunity *n.* a business venture which you might decide to invest in

investment philosophy *n.* the general set of principles or strategies that investors use to choose their investments such as quick profit, long-term growth or sustainability

investment-grade *adj. Investment-grade* securities are a fairly safe investment because they are likely to be repaid.

investor *n.* a person or organisation that invests money in order to make a profit

inward investment *n.* investment in an area, country, etc. from another area or country

irregularity *n.* not obeying the usually accepted legal or moral rules

J

joint and several liability *n.* when a number of different people or organisations are responsible both as group and individually for harm or injury they have caused

joint venture *n.* business activity in which two or more companies have invested together

judgement (also **judgment**) *n.* **1** a decision made by a court of law **2** an opinion formed or a decision made after careful thought

junk bond *n.* a bond with a high rate of interest, but with a high risk of not being repaid

jurisdiction *n.* the official right and power to make decisions about something

K

key accounting policy *n.* the main principles, rules and procedures followed in preparing and reporting a company's financial statements, which deal with matters such as consolidation of accounts, depreciation methods, goodwill, etc. and must be disclosed in the annual financial statements

L

late-cycle company *n.* a company in a market which takes time to react to changing economic conditions

lawsuit *n.* a charge, claim or complaint against someone that is made in a court of law by a private person or company, not by the police or state

legal challenge *n.* when a person or company tries to have an existing law changed in a court of law

legal debate *n.* a discussion or argument about whether a specific point of law is justified or how it should be applied

legal opinion *n.* an opinion about a specific point of law given by a legal expert, such as a judge or law lord in the UK

legal reform *n.* a change made to law so that it operates in a fairer, more effective way

legislation *n.* **1** a law or set of laws **2** the act of making laws

lender *n.* a person or organisation that lends people money

liability *n.* **1** a balance-sheet term to describe an amount of money owed by a business to a supplier or lender or the government **2** a legal obligation to settle a debt or pay compensation for causing damage to another person or company

limited liability company (Ltd) *n.* The owners of a *limited liability company* are only responsible for their company's debts up to a certain amount if it goes out of business and do not have to sell their personal assets to repay these debts.

limited liability partnership (LLP) *n.* a partnership in which some or all partners (depending on the law in that country) have limited liability. In an *LLP*, one partner is not responsible or liable for another partner's misconduct or negligence.

line of credit (also **credit line**) *n.* an arrangement with a bank for a loan or a number of loans

liquidity *n.* **1** cash **2** when investments can easily be bought and sold on a particular financial market **3** the ability of a company to make payments to employees and suppliers, interest payments to banks, etc. **4** the ability of a bank to pay back people and organisations that have put money in the bank and that want to take their money out

loan *n.* money borrowed from a bank, financial institution, person, etc. on which interest is usually paid to the lender until the loan is repaid

loss *n.* when a business spends more money than it receives in a particular period of time, or loses money in some other way

M

management accounts *n.pl.* summarised accounting data such as cashflow, profit and loss statement and balance sheet, prepared on a regular basis and presented to the managers of a company to help them make short-term decisions

management buyout *n.* when a company's top managers buy the company, or a part of the company, they work for

margin call *n.* when an investor who has borrowed money from a broker in order to buy shares through that broker (buying on margin) has to make up the margin deposit, which has been reduced by a fall in the price of the shares on which it is based, to the required minimum level

market performance *n.* the degree to which a particular market, such as retail, is profitable

market share *n.* the percentage of sales in a market that a company or product has

market value *n.* how much people would be willing to pay for something, rather than a value calculated in another way

market volatility *n.* when a market is changing quickly and suddenly, for example when the stock market is rising and falling without much warning

material inconsistency *n.* a significant difference between what the auditors believe to be a company's true financial state and the information given by its directors in the annual report

material misstatement *n.* false or missing information, whether caused by fraud (including deliberate misstatement) or error

meetings minutes *n.pl.* an official written record of what is said and decided at a meeting

merger *n.* when two or more companies join together to form a larger company

milestone *n.* a very important event in the development of something, such as a stage in company project or the company's history

minority investor *n.* an investor who holds less than half of a company's shares

mortgage lender *n.* a bank or other financial institution that lends money to help people and companies buy property

multinational company *n.* a company with offices, factories or business activities in many different countries

N

negligence *n.* failure to take enough care over something that you are responsible for, for which you may have to pay damages

net *adj.* A *net* amount of money is one that remains after things such as costs and tax have been taken away.

O

operating expenses *n.pl.* expenses relating to a company's normal operating activities rather than financial dealings such as stock-market trading

operating income *n.* income from a company's normal operating activities, not including exceptional items

operating profit *n.* profit relating to a company's normal activities of providing goods or services

option *n.* the right to buy or sell shares, bonds, currencies or commodities at a particular price within a particular period of time or on a particular date in the future

options position *n.* the amount of call or put options contracts you hold

order book *n.* **1** a book listing all the orders for goods or services a company has received **2** used to talk about the orders themselves

outsource v. If a company or organisation *outsources* its work, it employs another company to do it.

P

parent company n. a company that owns other companies

pay policy n. the way a company decides how much and in which way it pays its employees

peak n. a time when prices, shares, etc. reach their highest point or level

penalty n. **1** a punishment for breaking a law or rule **2** an amount of money someone has to pay if they do not keep to a legal agreement, especially an agreement with a bank or an insurance company

performance n. the degree to which a company, investment or financial market is profitable

performance driver n. a key element of a system that has a significant impact on its performance

politician n. someone who works in politics, especially an elected member of the government

portfolio of investments n. a collection of investments held by one person or company

preferential treatment n. when one person or company is given an advantage over another person or company

price speculation n. when goods, shares or property are bought in the hope that their value will increase so that they can be sold at a higher price, often quickly

private sector n. the industries and services that are not owned by the government

production n. **1** the process of making or growing things to be sold as products, usually in large quantities **2** an amount of something that is produced

professional liability n. the responsibility of a professional person such as an auditor or lawyer for damage or loss caused by the services or advice that they give

profit before tax n. a company's profit before tax has been taken away

proportion n. a part of a number or amount, considered in relation to the whole

proposal n. a plan or idea which is suggested formally to an official person

proposition n. **1** a business idea, offer or suggestion, for example a possible business deal **2** (US) a suggested change to the law of a state, which citizens vote on **3** a statement that consists of a carefully considered opinion or judgement

public limited company n. (UK) a limited company whose shares are freely sold and traded, with a minimum share capital of £50,000 and the letters *plc* after its name

public policy n. government-stated objectives relating to the health, morals and well-being of its citizens

public sector n. the companies, organisations and activities in an economy that are owned by the government

put option n. an option that allows you to sell shares at a specific price in the future, with the aim of making a profit, which you buy because you think prices will fall below that price

Q

qualified opinion n. a comment by an auditor that the accounts of a company give a true and fair view of its finances except in specified ways, for example that they show some things in a way that the auditor does not approve

R

real estate n. **1** land or buildings **2** the business of selling land or buildings

reasonable assurance n. a high degree of confidence by a person or company

recession n. a period of time when an economy or industry is doing badly and business activity and employment are increasing

regeneration n. the process whereby a town or area attracts investment to improve and renew it, replacing old, run-down buildings with new ones and building new community facilities, such as education and recreation facilities

> **regeneration target** an organisation, industry or region that is deliberately chosen to be improved and updated

regulator n. a person or organisation who is chosen by the government to be responsible for making sure that an industry or system works legally and fairly

regulatory authority n. a government body which is given responsibility by a specific law to ensure that the law is followed, for example by companies

regulatory barrier to trade n. a law in force in a country which makes trading between two countries more difficult or expensive, for example a tax on imports

regulatory reform n. changes to laws in a particular country

regulatory requirements n.pl. things which are necessary by law in a particular field, such as accounting

regulatory risk n. a risk to a particular business that it will lose money if regulatory authorities change specific rules which apply to business activities it has already engaged in

remedy n. **1** a way of dealing with a problem **2** a punishment

reserves n.pl. **1** money held by a bank and used to pay out money to customers when they ask for it. The amount that must be kept in this way is decided by government. **2** a company's profits from previous periods of time that have not been paid to shareholders

resignation n. when someone officially states that they want to leave their job or position

resolution n. an official decision or statement agreed on by two or more people or groups of people, often after a vote

retail deposits (also **core deposits**) n.pl. the money that savers put into banks and building societies

return on investment n. the profit on an investment, usually described as a percentage of the original amount invested

revenue n. money that a business or organisation receives over a period of time, for example from selling goods or services

reward n. money earned by an investment

risk n. **1** the possibility that a business will encounter a situation which will have a negative effect on its profits **2** the possibility that a person or business will not pay back a loan **3** the possibility that the value of an asset may go up or down on the stock market

risk factor n. something which poses a risk to a person, company or society

risk management n. **1** policies, procedures and practices which companies and organisations use in order to assess potential areas of risk in their operations, with the aim of minimising or eliminating them **2** the managing of investments in ways that produce as much profit as possible while limiting the danger of losses

S

savings n.pl. money that is kept in a bank to be used later, rather than spent

scam n. a clever but dishonest plan, usually to get money

securitise v. If a financial institution *securitises* loans, it buys the loans from lenders such as banks and issues bonds for a specific amount to a further set of investors. It makes regular payments to these investors from the repayments it receives from the people who originally took out the loans.

share capital *n.* money that a company has from investors who have bought shares

share price *n.* the price of a particular company's shares at a particular time

shareholders' equity *n.* the difference between the value of a company's assets and its liabilities, other than those to shareholders. In principle, this is what the company would be worth to shareholders if it stopped trading, its assets were sold and its debts were paid.

short seller *n.* a trader who agrees to sell a commodity, currency or security which they do not actually own at the time of sale, requiring the purchase of this asset in order to be able to sell it on

short squeeze *n.* a situation in which a lot of short sellers are trying to buy the shares they need to deliver to people who have agreed to buy them from the short sellers, causing prices to rise

skill *n.* an ability to do something well, especially because you have learned and practised it

stake *n.* the amount of money invested in a particular business

standard accounting practice *n.* a set of rules that a company must follow when reporting information on its financial statement. The *standard accounting practice* guidelines allow companies to be compared to each other because they have followed the same rules.

start-up capital *n.* the money which is required to finance a new business through the first years of its life

start-up company *n.* a company that has just been formed

state organisation *n.* an organisation which is run by the government

statutory accounts *n.pl.* (UK) accounts that must be prepared in a set format, prescribed by company law, and be published in the public domain and filed with the Registrar of Companies at Companies House

stock exchange (also **stock market**) *n.* an organised and regulated market where shares, bonds and notes are bought and sold so that entities such as companies and governments, for example, can raise capital. On modern exchanges, trades are conducted by phone and online, rather than by shouting orders over the trading floor.

stock-market index *n.* a list of market prices of groups of stocks, such as the FTSE 100 in the UK

stock-market regulator *n.* a person or organisation that is chosen by the government to be responsible for making sure that the stock market works legally and fairly

strategy *n.* a plan or series of plans for achieving an aim, especially success in business or the best way for an organisation to develop in the future

strengths *n.pl.* **1** the good qualities or abilities that someone or something has **2** the power or influence that a person or organisation/country has

subprime mortgage *n.* a residential mortgage issued to high-risk borrowers, such as those with a history of late payments or bankruptcy. A lot of defaults in the sector shook credit markets in 2008.

sum-of-the-parts basis *n.* a calculation showing whether the value of a company would be increased if it were split into separate business units and shares of stocks of the separate units were sold to the public

supply chain *n.* a system of organisations, people, technology, activities, information and resources involved in moving a product or service from the supplier to the customer. *Supply-chain* activities transform natural resources, raw materials and components into a finished product.

sustainability *n.* the act of preserving the world's natural resources for future generations. A fully sustainable industry would be one that had zero impact, or a positive impact, on the environment.

sustainable investment *n.* an investment which has as its objectives things such as absence of pollution, low environmental impact, and low and steady growth rather than a speedy and high return at the expense of the environment

T

taskforce *n.* a group formed for a short time to deal with a particular problem

tax rate *n.* the part of your income or the part of the price of something that you pay in tax, expressed as a percentage

taxation *n.* **1** the act or system of charging taxes **2** money collected from taxes

trading history *n.* data about the sales revenue of a company over a specified number of years

trading update *n.* information about a company's recent performance, given to the public

transaction *n.* **1** a transfer of cash that occurs between two or more parties and establishes a legal obligation **2** an occasion when a company buys or sells shares or bonds, for example, or exchanges them for other shares or bonds

transparency *n.* when rules, methods or business dealings are clear and easy to understand by everybody, rather than just a specialist

treasury *n.* **1** the government department in charge of the money that a country collects in taxes and from borrowing **2** the money that such a department spends

trend *n.* the general way in which a particular situation is changing or developing

true and fair view *n.* words used in a company's accounts by directors and auditors to show that they think the accounts give correct and complete information about a company's financial situation

V

values *n.pl.* the principles and practices that a business or organisation thinks are important and which it tries to follow

viability *n.* when a plan or method is judged to be able to work successfully

voluntary sector *n.* the part of society that does work for no pay

vote *v.* to show by marking a paper, electronic document or by raising your hand which person you want to elect or whether you support a particular proposal

W

watchdog *n.* an independent organisation responsible for making sure that companies in a particular industry or business do not do anything illegal

weakness *n.* **1** a lack of skill, power, success or influence **2** something that can be criticised easily

wholesale funding *n.* a debt method that banks use, rather than savers deposits, to finance operations such as lending money to customers.

workforce *n.* all the people who work in a particular country, industry or factory

Organisations and standards

Association of Chartered Certified Accountants (ACCA)
An international accounting organisation with over 300,000 members in more than 160 countries which was formed in 1904 as the London Association of Accountants

Auditing Practices Board
An organisation that sets standards of auditing with the objective of enhancing public confidence in the audit process and the quality and relevance of audit services in the public interest. Its remit has been extended to include responsibility for setting standards for auditors' integrity, objectivity and independence.

Chartered Institute of Management Accountants (CIMA)
An organisation that is internationally recognised as offering a financial degree for business, focusing on strategic business management. It was founded in 1919 as the Institute of Cost and Works Accountants.

European Central Bank
The central bank of the European Union, based in Frankfurt and responsible for setting interest rates, controlling the money supply, etc. of countries using the euro

European Commission
A central organisation of the European union with political and administrative responsibilities. It is directed by officials from member countries, each with a particular responsibility.

Financial Reporting Council (FRC)
A unified, independent regulator with a mission of promoting confidence in corporate reporting and governance in the UK. It and its subsidiaries play vital roles in the oversight and development of corporate governance standards in the UK.

Financial Services Authority (FSA)
An organisation that, in 1997, took control of regulation of the British financial services industry from the nine separate organisations which previously had been responsible for banking, insurance, etc.

Halifax Bank of Scotland (HBOS)
HBOS was formed by the 2001 merger of Halifax plc (a former building society) and the governor and company of the Bank of Scotland, making it a company of comparable size to the 'big four' UK retail banks, and the country's largest mortgage lender. Due to serious financial difficulties in 2008, it was taken over by the Lloyds Banking Group in January 2009.

Institute of Chartered Accountants in England and Wales (ICAEW)
The largest professional accountancy body in Europe

Institute of Chartered Accountants of Scotland (ICAS)
The world's first professional body of accountants, receiving its Royal Charter in 1854. It was the first to adopt the designation *Chartered Accountant* and the designatory letters *CA*.

International Accounting Standards Board (IASB)
An organisation with the aim of making a single set of high-quality, understandable and International Financial Reporting Standards (IFRSs) for general purpose financial statements

International Federation of Accountants (IFAC)
The global organisation for the accountancy profession. It works with its 157 members and associates in 123 countries and jurisdictions to protect the public interest by encouraging high-quality practices by the world's accountants.

International Financial Reporting Standards (IFRS)
Standards, interpretations and the framework for the preparation and presentation of financial statements adopted by the International Accounting Standards Board (IASB). Many of the standards forming part of IFRS are known by the older name of International Accounting Standards (IAS).

International Organisation of Securities Commissions (IOSCO)
A global co-operative of securities regulatory agencies that aims to establish and maintain worldwide standards for efficient, orderly and fair markets

International Standards on Auditing
Professional standards for the performance of financial audit of financial information. These standards are issued by the International Federation of Accountants through the International Auditing and Assurance Standards Board.

Securities and Exchange Commission
In the USA, a government organisation which controls the way in which bonds and shares are traded and makes sure investment arrangements are legal. The organisation that does this in the UK is the Financial Services Authority.

The Prince of Wales's Accounting for Sustainability Project
A project which is bringing organisations together to develop practical tools to enable environmental and social performance to be better connected with strategy and financial performance, and thereby embedded into day-to-day operations and decision-making

Treasury Select Committee
Sometimes referred to as the *House of Commons Treasury Committee*, this is a select committee of the House of Commons in the Parliament of the United Kingdom. The committee examines the expenditure, administration and policy of HM Treasury, with all of its agencies and associated bodies, including HM Revenue and Customs, the Bank of England, the Financial Services Authority, the Royal Mint, etc.

World Bank
A group of five organisations based in Washington, DC, and linked to the United Nations that gives financial help and advice to developing countries

World Trade Organisation
An organisation that was formed in 1995 to control trade agreements between countries and to set rules on international trade. It replaced GATT.